Astrology & Romance

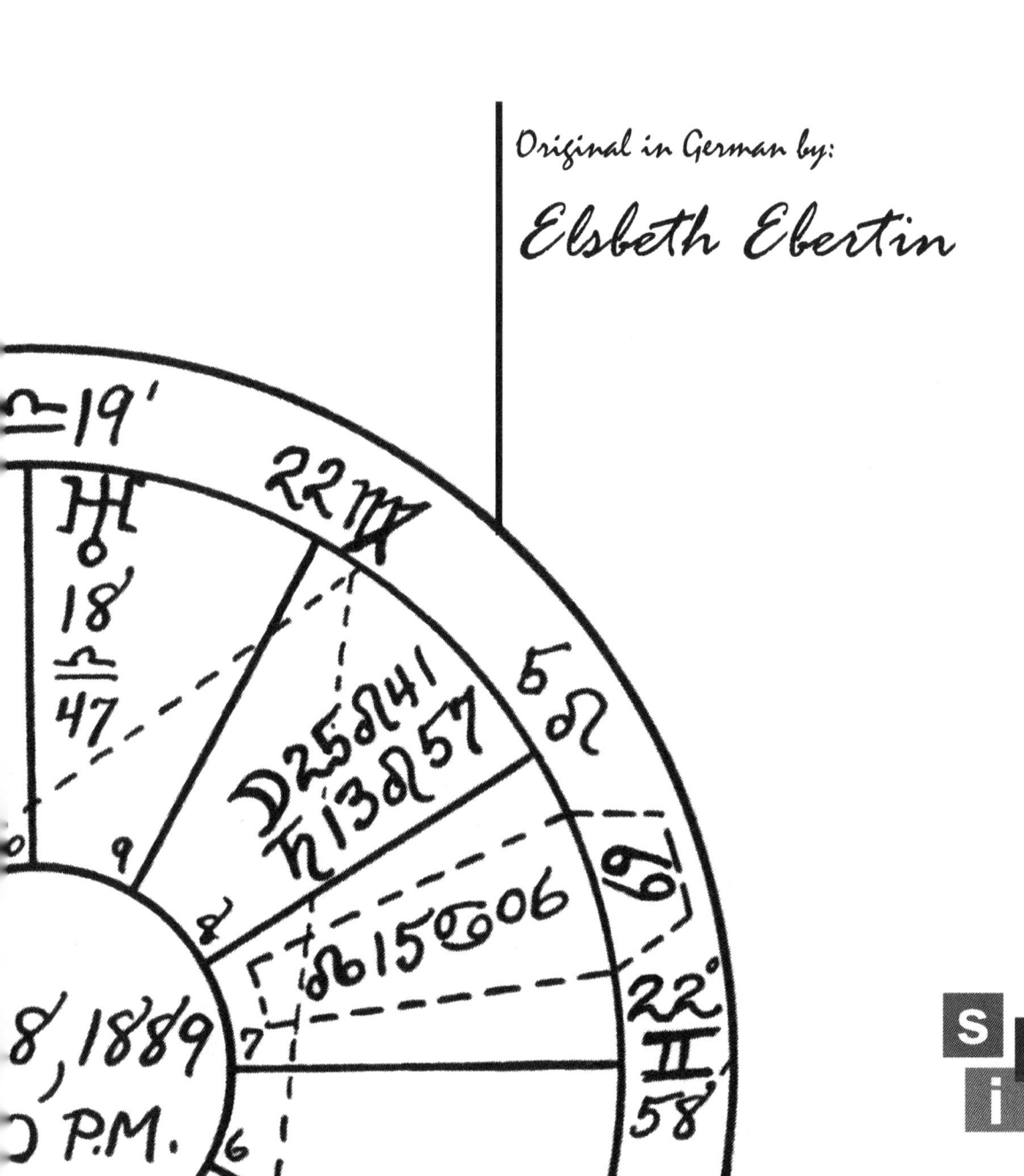

Astrology & Romance

Original in German by:

Elsbeth Ebertin

Cover Design: **Greg McNamara**
Layout Editor: **Hori Hashimoto**

Portions Copyright ©2003 by Standard Publications, Inc.
Standard Publications, Inc.
Urbana, IL 61801

All rihgts reserved. No part of this book may be reproduced, stored in a retrieval system, or transmitted, in any form or by any means, electronic, mechanical, photocopying, recording, or otherwise, without prior written permission from the publisher.

The publisher of this book makes no warranty of any kind, express or implied, as to the fitness of this book for any purpose. The publisher shall not be held liable in any event for incidental or consequential damages in connection with, or arising out of, the furnishing, performance, or use of this information.

The publisher offers discounts on this book when ordered in bulk quantities.

ISBN 0-9709788-5-5

Library of Congress 2002107582

Printed in the United States of America

Standard Publications, Incorporated

To All That Know Love!

Table of Horoscope Charts

Chart No.	Page
2	19
3	21
4	22
5	24
6	27
7	28
8	29
9	33
10	41
11	42
12	43
13	64
14	65
15	71
16	76
17	89
18	109
19	113
20	117
21	121
22	123

Wolfgang von Goethe's handwriting from "Egmont"
(Translation follows)

Introduction

For many years I contemplated writing a book about "Astrology and Romance"; ten years ago I was fully resolved to do so, and in several of my former annuals, entitled, "A Vision into the Future," reference was made to this new publication.

The continuous flood of communications coming from the readers of my various publications, as well as delays of every description, never permitted me, nevertheless, to complete the work as planned. There were other important tasks; other actual events that claimed my first attention, and so there was nothing left for me to do but to collect a wealth of material, and time and again to observe how planets also act upon the love affairs of men.

In the end I consoled myself with the thought that the theme of love never is out of date, and that it would be no calamity for the book to appear later, as soon as there would be sufficient time to cull from the fullness and wealth of material that which was best adapted.

Love, after all forever remains news!

To this day, and for all days to come a quotation from the old master, Goethe (see facsimile of handwriting, previous page), holds good for all that know love:

> *"Full of joy and sorrow*
> *To be wrapped up in thought,*
> *To hang and to falter*
> *In pain suspended,*
> *A shout of joy to the heavens,*
> *Sorrowful unto death,*
> *Happy alone*
> *Is the soul which loves."*

Yes, indeed, "happy alone is the soul which loves," and accordingly, every one who has found the happiness of love, and moreover, he who hopes to find it would want to know something about his fortunes *as they are written in the stars.*

During the last few years, perhaps, and since I had made a pertinent suggestion in my volume on "Religion and Love" (1919), other books may have been published on the same theme, however, I believe that these have a different treatment of the subject.

At first I published in the World-Rhythm Calendar for 1926 an excerpt of this brochure, in which I described especially the planet positions of the 7th house of a native, as that would be significant for love and marriage.

This volume presents a large number of ancient and modern Astrological observations and rules of interpretation, together with more than 20 interesting horoscopes of males and females, such as the following: *happy and unhappy lovers and married people, such as married and have been divorced several times, those that anxiously but vainly hope for their romance, chaste virgins and bachelors, and such as have been spoiled in a tragical manner, and have died.*

I should like to remark that I am not writing the book for scientists and expert astrologists, who may have collected study material of their own; it was my endeavor to rather compile from very old volumes, beginning from the 16th century unto modern times, that which may be used today and may be elucidated with examples of our times. Whoever of the learned men will take exception to my inserting here and there some poetry and philosophy

Introduction

between astrological explanations, instead of bringing mathematics and complicated arithmetical problems which the layman would not understand anyway, but rather to offer something to *those* esteemed readers of both sexes for whom it would be too difficult to penetrate into the sphere of astrology; whoever objects, let him lay this book aside, and stay with his gray folios.

With this book I am chiefly concerned to place something into the hands of the educated laymen, of all lovers of the nation, that are not in the position to purchase expensive works, something that will allow them to gain an insight into their fortunes and love affairs, and to enable-them to know themselves through the comparison of examples.

The volume will of course prove to be particularly interesting for those who already have a horoscope sketch, since they now can refer to the respective page to see what this and that planet position means. Good interpretations of horoscopes are very hard to obtain.

Thus I trust that this very book, treating as it does of the inaccessible stars, as well as of the joys and woes of love, will cause my attentive readers of both sexes to realize much of what was to them only a dark premonition, and that the book will be especially instructive and useful to all lovers.

At the Beginning of February, 1926.

ELSBETH EBERTIN.

Weinberg (Württemberg) vei Heilbronn a.N.

Powers of Stars
and the Yearning for Love

Love is the star of poetry,
Love is the heart of life,
And who has completed the song of love,
Has achieved eternity

—Friedrich Rueckert.

There is an eternal sound in the words STAR and LOVE, a cosmic connection of the sounds of the universe, an interrelated oscillation which unconsciously but harmoniously connects the two terms. If you will inquire into that sound, you will arrive at indefinite premonitions. Perhaps one might say, they both possess the same glow, a power baffling description, a quaint attraction amidst a mysterious longing; it is difficult, however, to put into concise words that which has been experienced and felt about the power of the stars and about love, and to decode the peculiar connection of both.

Nevertheless, the interrelations between the activities of the stars and the sentiments of men are far more intricate than most men think. Many people refuse to believe there are fluid energies of the universe, or astral currents, or a warp and woof between heaven and earth, and much less would suppose that love affairs are influenced by the stars or some higher powers.

It sounds so improbable to them, and still it is the most natural thing in the world.

But how shall we give account to those who fail to see in themselves any trace of that mysterious fluid working between the energies of the stars and the sentiments of love? Would it be sufficient to quote that oft repeated word of Goethe, "If you do not feel it, you will never achieve it?"

Is it possible that men whose minds run in a purely materialistic course can believe in anything at all except they see it or grasp it? Surely, an effort must then be made to draw on other comparisons and arguments. There is Robert Fuchs-Liska and his brochure treating on the rays of the stars, entitled, "Laymen's Astrology," which has the following:

> "Perhaps we should call it an urge, a force of an electrical nature, superinduced by extremely delicate currents. We certainly cannot perceive these radiations with our senses, that is, not by means of the eye, the ear, the taste, the touch, the smell. However, that which we call nerves, has a capacity for feeling the oscillations of stars, they resist, or react favorably. Externally we react through body appearances; certainly through physical ailments. Our inner man, the soul or spirit, perceives such impressions of the planetary radiations as we do not notice at all. Thus the character may change from good to bad, and vice versa. Our actions are accordingly, and thus we prepare our own fortune, or create a misfortune. The dissonant or consonant sounds in us continue – often for a long time, sometimes for a day only, but never without a preparation – the strings vibrate very softly, the sound becomes extenuated; the vibrations increase until they have reached their highest degree of oscillation. That which we do, receive, or give accordingly, is the reaction of the harmony or disharmony within us. When there is harmony, we achieve for ourselves enduring happiness, or happiness for some special day; when disharmony prevails we construe a chain of disastrous events, or at least appearing disastrous for a day, these events being linked to one another through brief interruptions."

I believe these matters should no longer be too difficult to understand in our days of radio activity, inasmuch as the transcendency of sound and radio waves is something self evident.

Powers of Stars

Nor should it be difficult to understand that the stars also shed invisible energies and pervade our affections, move and excite our heartstrings, and produce a happy or joyous mood at times when affinities become associated, or whenever some one through the ruling of fate finds his other self in person, the related soul.

We shall quote Friedrich Schiller at this instance:

"Such is love's sacred bolt of the gods,
Which darts into the soul, and strikes, inflames.
When affinity finds the affinity
There is no resistance, and no choice,
Man does not sever, what Heaven has bound together."

Indeed, the invisible and mysterious energies in the universe, which bring lovers together that never can leave one another, these energies are more powerful than any other law.

There are thousands of treatises on love; there has been penned in song in all variations by poets of ancient and modern times, beginning with Walther von der Vogelweide in his "Minnesang" to the folk song and the well dramatized works of our generation.

From the remote ages people spoke of the stars that influence one's fortunes, they investigated their bearing upon the inhabitants of this orbit and upon things mundane. Unto whom, however, is bequeather the boon of love? Who is perfectly happy? Of many thousands, few only are contented, and even in marriages that appear to be well mated there is disharmony after a space of time, or some degree of alienation which at first was not considered possible. There is, of course, a difference in all things the happy hours may predominate in marriage, or the thorns and thistles of discord may destroy all the happiness that had existed. Most people have no idea as to where that sudden reversal of sentiment, or the gloomy moods, should come from after the first peaceful weeks or years. They do not know that there are invisible powers at work to destroy the erstwhile peace, the enjoyment of happiness, and that cosmic oscillations exert a baneful influence.

Accordingly, much indeed depends on the conjunction

of stars in the horoscope of lovers as well as other aspects predominating, whether the retroactive factors are a destructive or a beneficial force.

For one who has the timely opportunity to compare the horoscope of lovers, there are astrological laws which enable one to find out whether or not, according to the mutual activity of the stars, there is a possibility for permanent happiness and for a harmonious marriage, or whether there soon would be interference.

Too often, alas, erotic sensations are mistaken for love, and the first whirl of the senses vanishes as fast as it has appeared.

There is, of course, a minute difference between erotic sensations as joined together with a mutual understanding of mind and soul, and sensuality, which merely consists in satisfying menial desires, or giving vent to the burning passion.

In the former case, when minds understand one another, when there are common interests, and souls agree, these factors prevailing, it is likely that the harmony in love and marriage will be lasting rather than that persons are attracted to one another through sensuality and external matters. In the latter instance a first spell will very soon be followed by frigid relations and a somber sobriety. When these people have satisfied their sexual desires, they have nothing to give to one another, they easily tire of one another, and, being originally sensual, they now abhor, detest, and even hate each other. With the aid of astrology it may be ascertained whether or not two persons harmonize, not merely in a sensual manner, but also in soul and mind. To this end horoscopes may be compared, as I shall show in the next chapter.

Aspects will be discovered that are most contradictory, and there are factors in many horoscopes of lovers which prove to be attractive as well as repelling.

In this respect Friedrich Schiller said:

Powers of Stars

"Heaven has not only roses, but also thorns,
Blest thou art, when they do not injure thy garland,
That which Venus has tied together, who brings happiness,
Mars, the star of unhappiness, may soon tear asunder."

At times a premonition of some impending disaster is weighing heavily upon the young love, as though evil days are already casting their shadows. In most cases only one of the lovers will scent the disaster, and its inexplicable sorrow is foreboding a sudden separation.

There is also a lyrical poet of our day, Heinrich Schmidt-Hoffmann, who realizes that often the sword of Damocles is hovering over two lovers. He says in his poems of the starry night:

"Two lovers
Held each other in close embrace,
And kissed each other
Softly and long
Amidst the charms of midnight;
Alas, little could they know
That a hostile star
Was hovering over them
And from his chalice of sorrow
Drop upon drop
Softly, quite softly
Did he pour upon them."

Thus in poetic fashion the manner is told in which stars act upon loving hearts, changing joy into sorrow. However, the poet adds cheerfully:

"Little man, little man,
Why are you wringing your hands
Just because a planet has wounded you?
Be happy because of the scars!
Whoever has the most and worst,
I have said that for some time,
He is the warrior most pleasing to God,
He is a hero,

*A victorious hero
Of the eternal Lord."*

Accordingly, none of the esteemed readers, none of the ladies reading this, should lose courage as they study and compare life fortunes described in this book on the basis of the Zodiacal signs, and discover that from their own horoscope no particular happiness is indicated in their romance. Nor should they be afraid of the battles of life.

Many things at first look much worse than they are in reality, or will be. Or, inasmuch as we are living in critical times, troubles are borne easier when one is already expecting them. In the final analysis we ought not forget that we are here to fight, and that severe disappointments and strokes of evil fortune are necessary in life, for the development and purification of the soul.

Many a person, in whose horoscope there is a preeminence of restrictive or threatening aspects (Chart No. 3) might not be able to stand up under some catastrophe or some stroke of ill fortune, unless he has previously passed through a school of great sorrow, and has become acquainted with many a sorrow each in its turn.

However, before I say any more of *aspects,* that is, of stars mutually viewing each other, I must here insert for the benefit of laymen who thus far have not read any astrological works, what is meant by a horoscope, or life mirror, and how to glance over a horoscope that has been completed by a mathematician or astrologer, and is now ready for reference, as the charts of this book, to enable the reader to decipher the foremost configurations himself.

The horoscope, meaning a view of the hour, or the configuration of the stars at the time of a birth, may be likened to a clock of heaven, reflecting human fate in large dimensions, whereas the incidents of human life must be ascertained through the computation of important directions and profections of the stars.

The horoscopes reproduced in this volume with their

peculiar configurations show in a measure merely that which with respect of character, the fortunes of love and marriage, has already taken place, or still is to be expected. *When* certain events will occur, will, of course, require exact computations in each case, which only an expert astrologist can make.

The circular division of a chart of heaven, together with the respective zodiacal signs, comprises 360 degrees of the zodiac, which surrounds the earth.

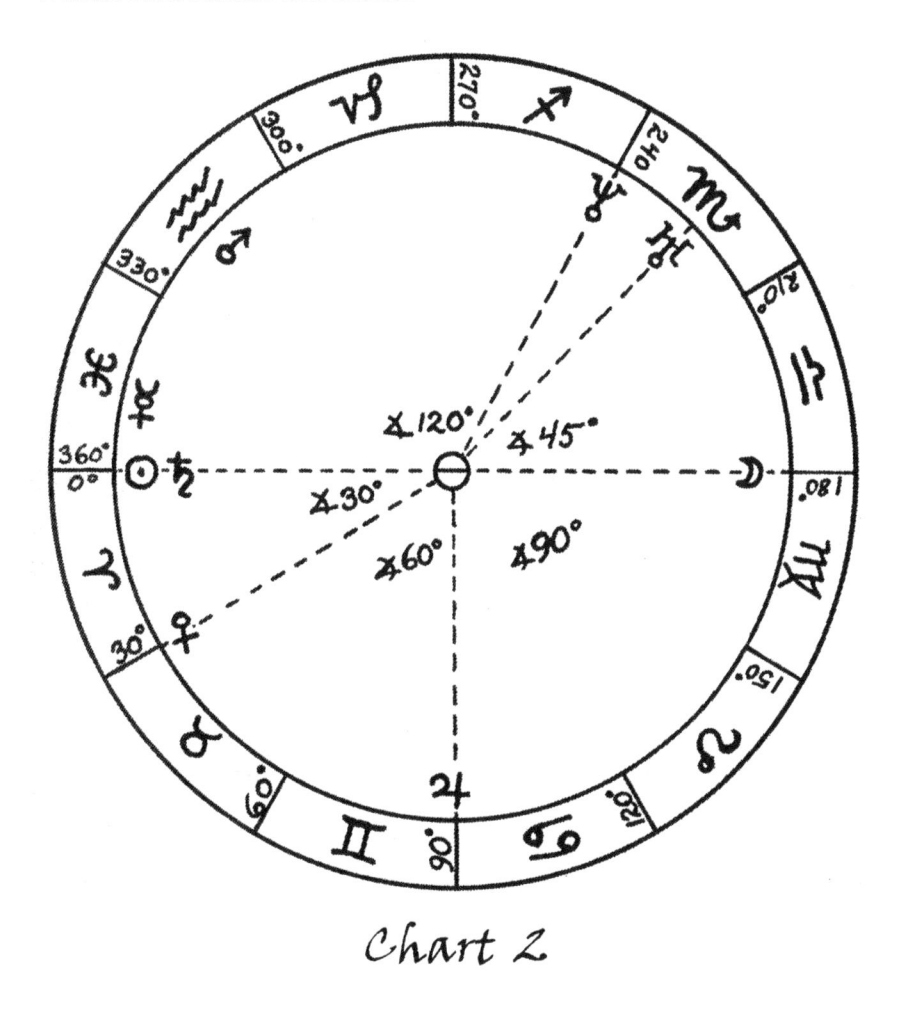

Chart 2

The names of the 12 zodiacal signs, each denoting 30 degrees, and connecting with each other, are as follows:

Degrees	Sign	Planet
0 - 30	Aries	Mars
30 - 60	Taurus	Venus
60 - 90	Gemini	Mercury
90 - 120	Cancer	Moon
120 - 150	Leo	Sun
150 - 180	Virgo	Mercury
180 - 210	Libra	Venus
210 - 240	Scorpio	Mars
240 - 270	Sagittarius	Jupiter
270 - 300	Capricorn	Saturn
300 - 330	Aquarius	Uranus
330 - 360	Pisces	Neptune & Jupiter

The extension or the size of the various houses, or of the 12 sectors of a horoscope that is mathematically exact, as the various horoscope charts from No. 3 to No. 22 will show, does not coincide with the degrees of the zodiacal signs, but is governed by the geographical location of the place of birth. One sector of a horoscope, for instance, as may be seen from the respective charts, may extend over several zodiacal degrees, as they are indicated in the outer circle.

(Now take a view of No. 3, of April 11, 1877.) Here the first house extends over the signs Aquarius, Pisces, and over the first degrees of the sign Aries.

At another horoscope (compare Chart No. 9 of May 13, 1893) the first house comprises only 15 degrees, the second half of the sign of Cancer.

Seldom only the beginning of a house point coincides completely with the beginning of a zodiacal sign, as in the horoscope No. 11, of June 14, 1888, which lies on the dividing line between the last degree of Virgo and the greater portion of the sign

Libra; still more exact is the coincidence of the ascendant 0 degree of Capricorn with the first house point in the horoscope No. 10, of August 1, 1893.

Every heaven area, or every house of the horoscope, has its own meaning, which I must describe here, so that every reader may try to know the fundamental traits of his character as well as of that of his female friend.

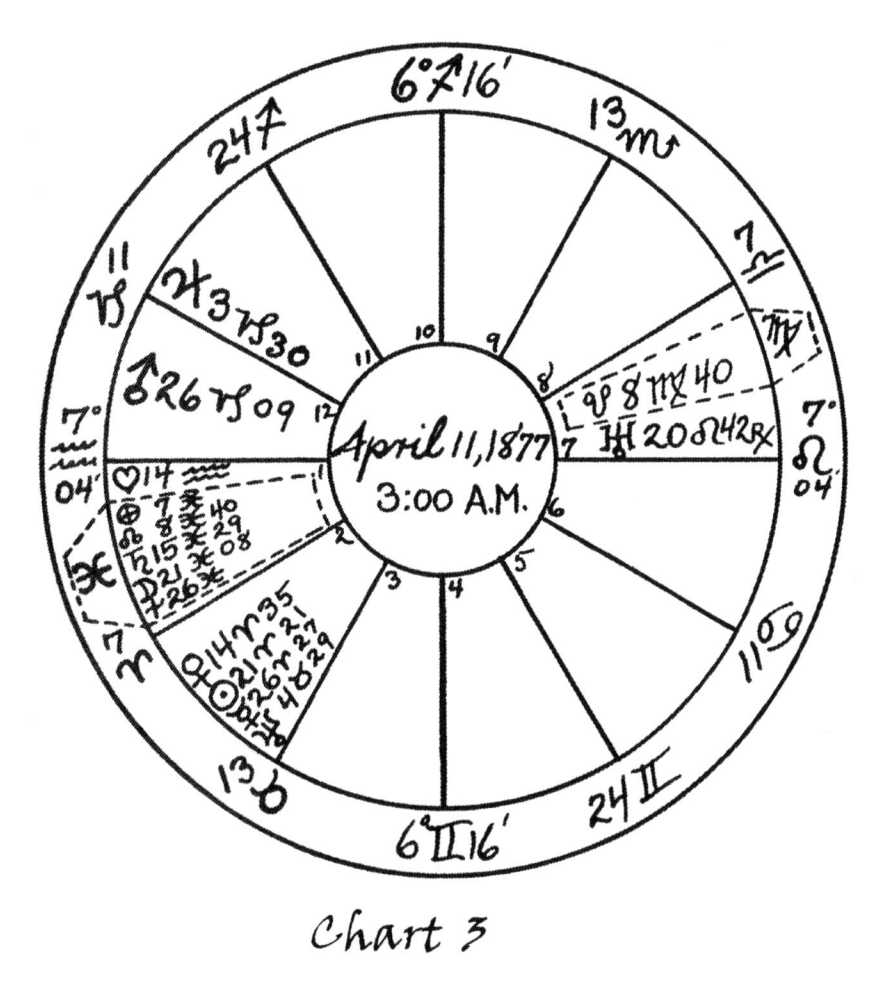

Chart 3

The first house describes character, personal inclinations, passions, as well as the fundamentals of fortune. If the first house of a horoscope extends over several signs, and accordingly is ruled over by various planets (as in No. 3), it may be assumed that there is an abundance of talents and versatility.

The second house, which connects with the first under the earth, tells of the financial standing, whether or not the native lives his life amidst wealth, for instance, when covered by the beneficent rays of Jupiter, or whether the person will labor under want and misery, whenever an evil star sheds its rays upon the second house, as for instance Neptune (see Chart No. 21).

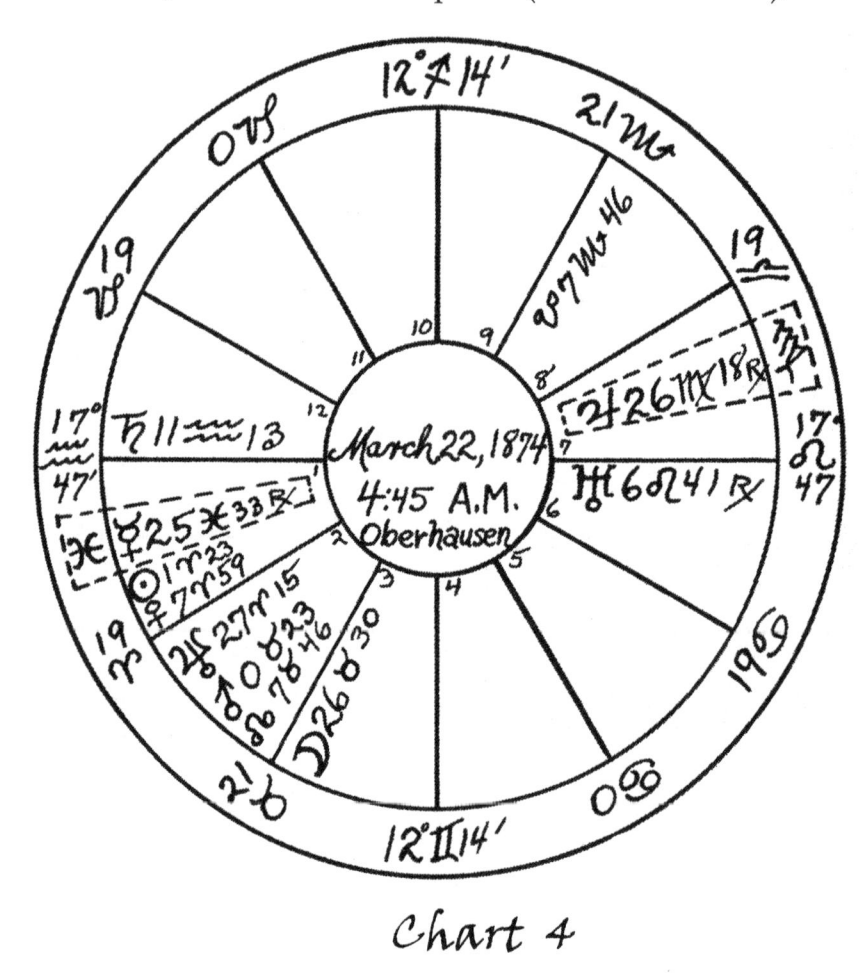

Chart 4

The third house informs one chiefly of interests of the mind, of relatives, brothers and sisters, short journeys, removals, letters, documents, neighborhood. Sun or Venus, with their beneficent rays, indicate much of mind progress, a good understanding with relatives, whereas unfavorable planets signify much trouble and altercation in the matters referred to.

The fourth house of the horoscope usually informs about the parents, the homestead, home country, as well as concerning conditions governing the native at the end of his life. When there are no planets present in the said houses, the position of the planet governing the respective zodiacal sign will determine.

Saturn in the fourth house (see No. 9), just to quote one example, usually causes much sorrow during the course of life, as to real estate, dangers accruing from severe strokes of fortune, or poverty in old age. (The person in question has for instance thoughtlessly sold a grist mill, the inheritance of his father, shortly before inflation, and since that time has been troubled financially.)

The fifth house of the horoscope is significant for joys and happy events of life; it will give directions as to amusements, gains or losses at play, when there are favorable or unfavorable planets in the house respectively. It also allows of deductions as to children and coming generations. Venus in the fifth house shows a propensity for acting rather prematurely in romance, nevertheless, also a faculty for the beautiful, for jollification, for theaters, art, music and song, for things that make life enjoyable. Jupiter's presence in the fifth house temporarily promises good fortune at games, when rays are favorable, or a sudden influx of money by means of protection or income through teaching, through success in art or literature. (See Chart No. 5.)

The sixth house will admit of conclusions regarding the conditions of the body, the health status, work, and dealing with subjects and servants. As the sixth house is well occupied by planets, that signifies a life replete with work, or a large working field. (See Charts No. 5 and 16.)

When Saturn is at the point of the sixth house, that will be a serious matter, at times there are hard battles, diseases must be overcome. Venus and Mercury usually indicate facetiousness in dealing with people of one's environment. Mars in the sixth house is less favorable, and will impair health; the Sun in the sixth house likewise. If the Sun sends his rays counter to Uranus, that will produce conditions of fear or sudden catastrophes, which may cause death. (See Chart No. 16, the horoscope of a female worker who had met her death at a catastrophal fire.)

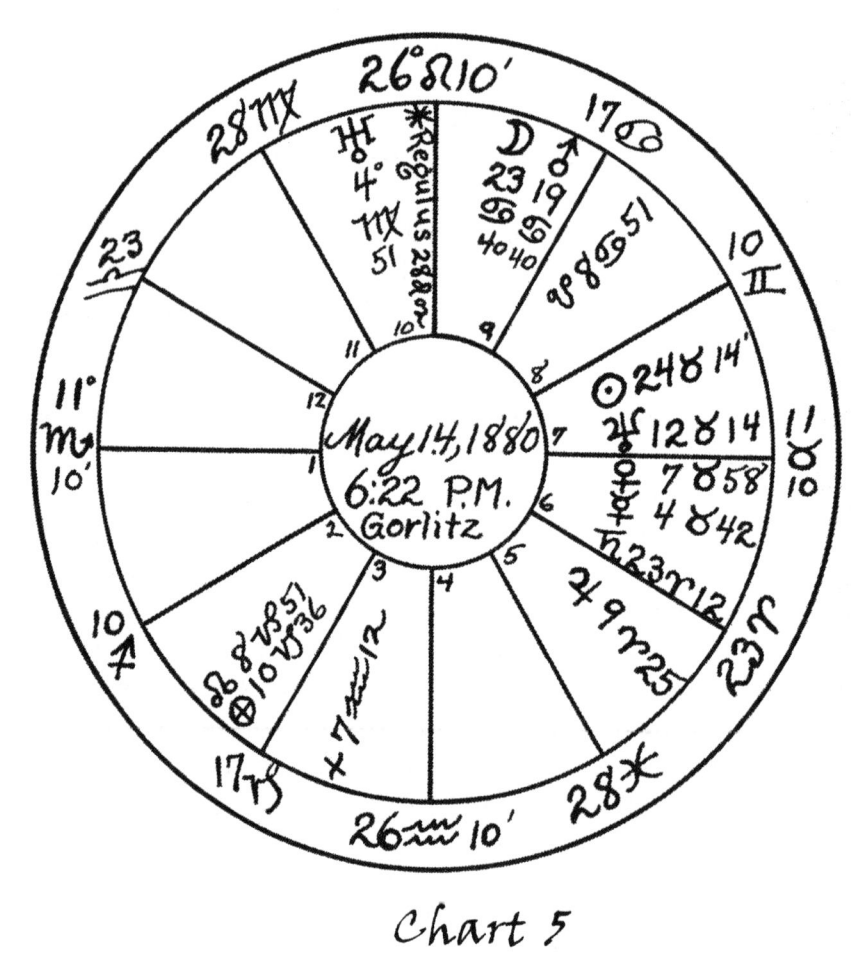

Chart 5

The seventh house of the horoscope reveals affairs of love and marriage, and furnishes information about partners and syndicates, concerning friends and foes, concerning public offices, and negotiations of every description. Since this volume deals with astrology and love, I shall offer various observations regarding the same, indicating the significance of all planets in this house. For the other houses it will be possible to make brief reference only of the meaning of the planets, and it will be necessary for me to reserve a more explicit description of all configurations for a later and more voluminous work.

The eighth house discloses secrets of the native or of his family, gives information about legacies, inheritance, the dower of the wife, the wealth of the husband, and at death also about the cause of death for the native. Many planets in the eighth house are not favorable for earthly happiness.   (Charts No. 19 and 21.)

The ninth house allows for judgment regarding the intellectual and moral qualities of the native and states whether or not he is about to travel extensively by land or by sea, in general, a change of location. If there are several planets in the ninth house it is an indication of many sided activities, which make travel necessary, whether one is so willing or not. See also Chart No. 5, showing the Moon and Mars, and Chart No. 11, showing Neptune, Venus, and Sun in the sign of Gemini, and others.

The tenth house is significant for the occupation, the social status, the power of the native, and shows glory, honor, achievements, but also dishonor, the failure and decadence of the person, according to the respective rays. Mars in the tenth house is usually unfavorable for the fortunes of the parents (Chart No. 21), and causes many battles and difficulties in one's calling.

The eleventh house decides about the general fortune or misfortune, about success, protection, gains; it also reveals the character of the friends, and whether others are harmful or beneficial. Jupiter, for instance, in the eleventh house, when rays are favorable, (see Chart No. 18 of the horoscope of Nov. 3, 1904), indicates valuable friendships in higher circles. The Moon, also in the eleventh house, is favorable (Chart No. 11).

The twelfth house of a horoscope reveals to us, according to its zodiacal signs and planetary positions, whether the native has many adversaries and enemies, and at what time. It also shows whether or not there is danger of conflicting with the courts, lawsuits, verdicts of guilty, a lengthy stay in closed buildings, in jail, in insane asylums, hospitals, a stay at some sanitorium, detention house; in general, a temporary seclusion from the world. Mars or Uranus in the twelfth house signify many enemies. (Charts No. 16 and 20.)

After giving a brief survey of what is to be expected of a

horoscope for the course of life, I shall now try to explain, with the aid of Chart No. 2, how to compute the distance of the planets from one another, so that any one who has horoscope charts may determine whether the harmonious or the disharmonious aspects predominate in his horoscope, and which aspects of the stars coincide with those of the lover and presage the good. Carefully examine again Chart No. 2.

This chart shows a circle divided into 360 degrees, which again is subdivided into 12 sectors. Beginning with degree 0 from the cross cut to the left, one will find the 12 zodiacal signs put down in order, beginning from the signs of Aries and Taurus to the sign of Pisces, which end in the 360th degree of this circle. All sectors are of equal size, so that the distance of the planets from each other may easily be determined.

To the left in the corner in 0 degree of Aries we see the symbol of the Sun, and closely aside of it the symbol of Saturn. When two heavenly bodies are so close to one another, as in the spring cusp in 0 degree of Aries, that is called a *conjunction* (coming together). A similar conjunction of Sun and Saturn we may find in the horoscope chart No. 19; however, several planets may at the same time come together in one sign.

Opposite to these two planets in Chart No. 2, at a distance of exactly 180 degrees, we see the symbol of the Moon. Such a contraposition of bodies of heaven is called *opposition* (counter ray). The elect electro-magnetic tension under this planetary position is very strong, and those people in whose horoscopes there are several of these oppositions of planets, will not have an easy time of it to always live at peace with their fellowmen. They will also learn to know of adverse situations, discussions, many separations and adversities.

The opposition is very acute in the horoscope charts Nos. 4, 6, 9, and 13. At a distance of 30 degrees each of the Sun and of Saturn in Chart No. 2 we find the planet Venus. This distance at an angle of 30 degrees is called a half sextile, or semi-sextile. It extends over a zodiacal sign. Likewise we have a semi-sextile when a planet is in the middle of a sign at the 15th degree and some other planet is at a distance of about 30 degrees in the following sign. See for instance such a one in Chart No. 5. Saturn 23 Aries, Sun 24 Taurus. Even from the 31st to 33rd degree is taken for a semi-sextile, since every planet has a circumference of at least 4-7 degrees.

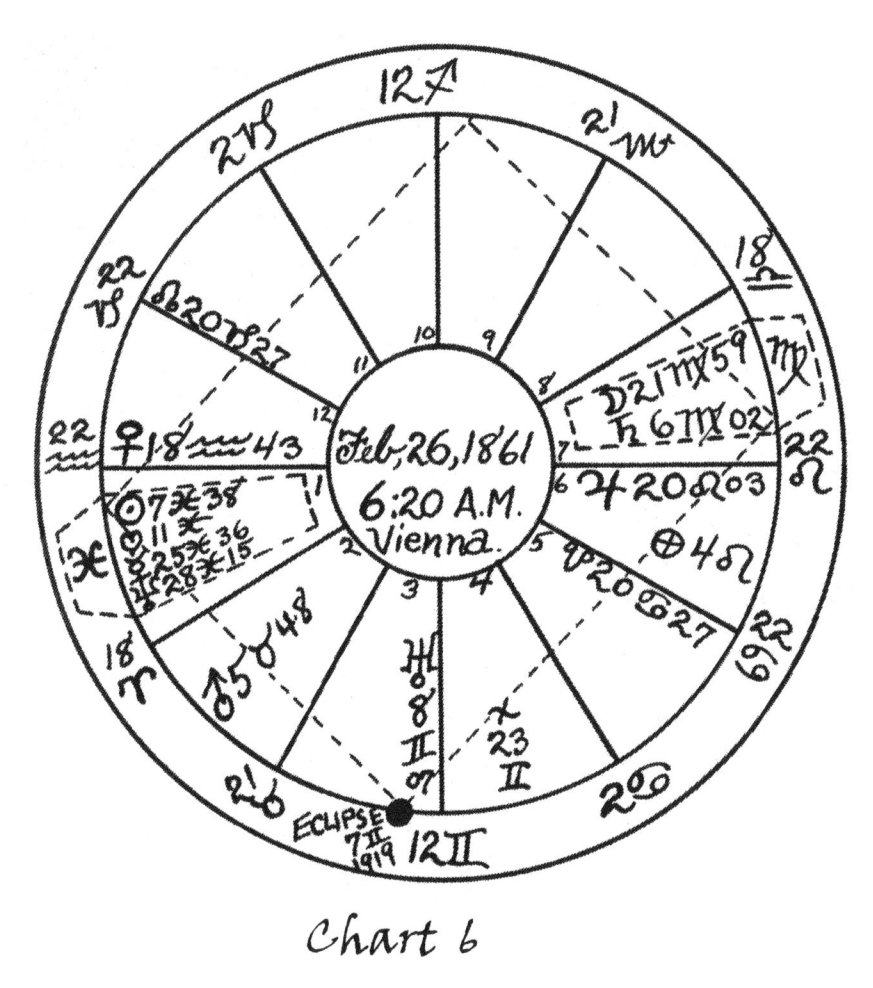

Chart 6

Counting from the 30th degree in Chart No. 2, to which I must always refer because it is better understood thus, at Aries, where Venus is located, for 60 degrees onward, we arrive at 30 degrees Gemini to the position of Jupiter, and we thus have a semi-sextile of two planets. This aspect, or the mutual facing of two planets, is generally thought of as favorable, unless their good effect is not hampered by cross currents.

Next we see in No. 2 at a distance of exactly 90 degrees from Jupiter the Moon at the space of three zodiacal signs. This difference in length at the space of 90 degrees is called a *quartile*. One could draw an exact square from the cusps of the corner houses, to contact the location of several planets, as it is marked in the horoscope of Chart No. 6. These quartiles have been termed evil from the ages, and "corners of disgust."

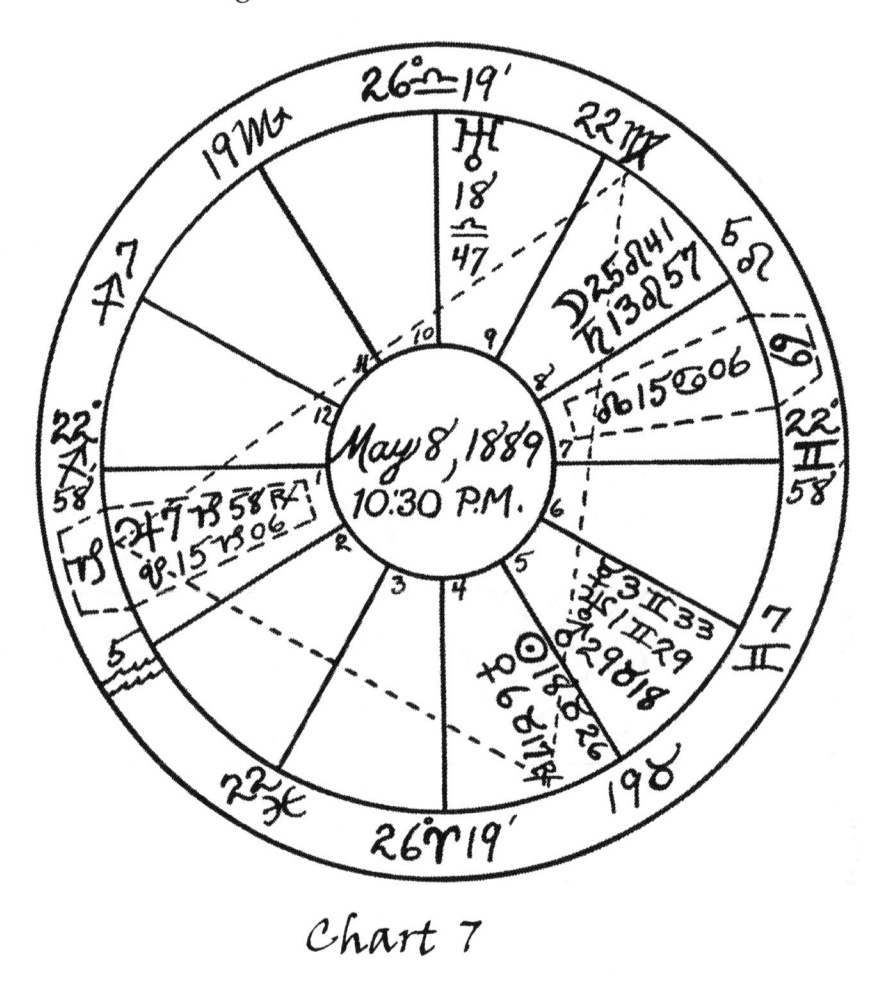

Chart 7

People whose horoscopes contain quartiles of influential planets, as in Charts 6, 20, and 21, must bear much adversity, living conditions will be greatly hampered, and they are subject to certain limitations, especially at times when these critical spaces are contacted by influential planets.

Powers of Stars

29

In Chart No. 2 the Moon does not only form a quartile with Jupiter at a distance of 90 degrees, but also an opposition to Saturn and to the Sun, so that several critical aspects work together.

If we proceed onward for 45 degrees from the Moon located in the 180th degree, we find in the middle of the sign Scorpio, Uranus. This space between two heavenly bodies is called semi-quartile, and it is not as significant as the quartile, but its action is unfavorable rather than favorable.

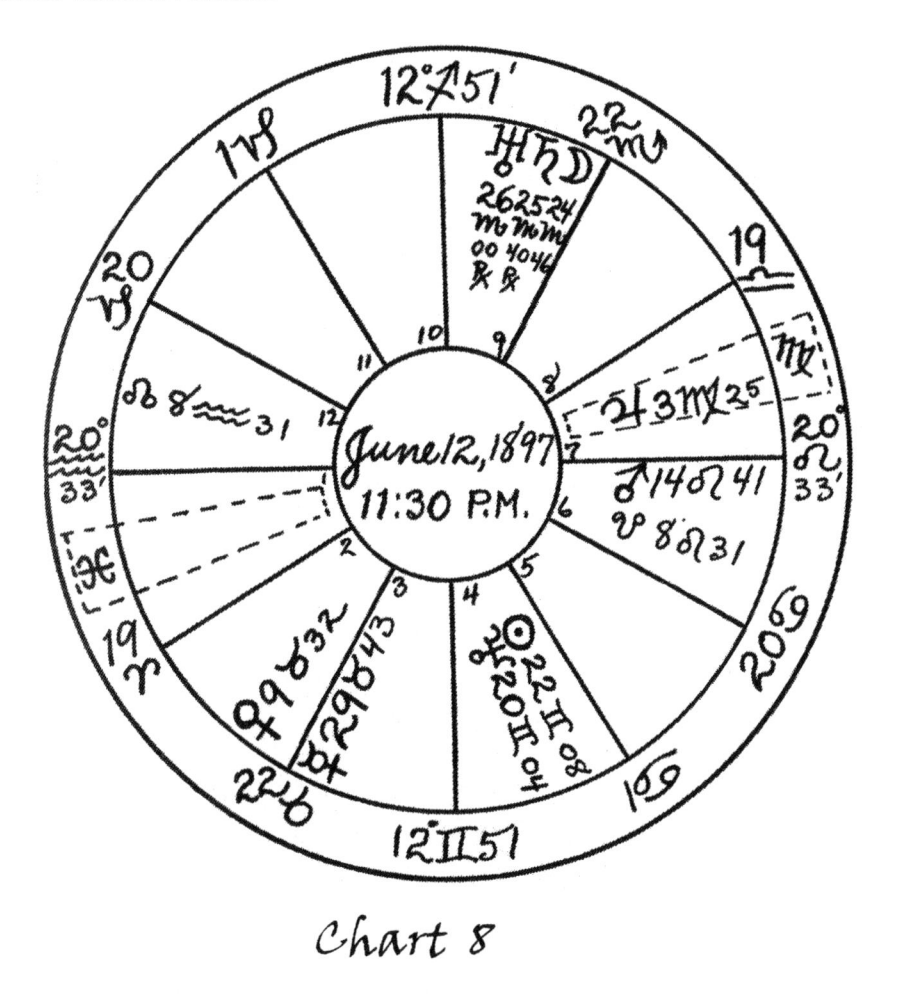

Chart 8

The best aspect is formed by a distance of two planets at the space of 120 degrees, as we find it in Chart No. 2, beginning from Neptune in the 240th degree of the zodiac, or 0 degree Sagittarius to the Sun or to Saturn.

Such a *triplicity*, which extends over four complete zodiacal signs, or 120 degrees, is considered harmonious and bringing happiness. We find such a trigon of two favorable planets -- marked by a triangle, in the Charts of the horoscopes of two persons *happily married,* in the Charts 7 and 8. The two planets Jupiter and Venus, which are significant for a happy marriage, are located in both horoscopes in the trigon (triplicity), and also in good alternative action for the horoscope of the marriage partner. At the birthday of the husband, May 8, 1889, his chief planet Jupiter stood at 7 degrees Capricorn, not only in triplicity to Venus 6 degrees Taurus in the fourth house in his own horoscope, but also in triplicity to Venus 9 degrees Taurus in the horoscope of the beloved wife. Her Jupiter in the 7th house of her horoscope again forms a triplicity, not only to Venus of her own horoscope in the 2nd house, but also a triplicity to Jupiter in the horoscope of the husband 7 degrees, nearly 8 degrees Capricorn. A difference of 3 or 4 degrees from the exact aspect location does not alter the computation, as has already been said, since every planet is active beyond several degrees. In these two horoscopes, No. 7 and No. 8, accordingly, Jupiter and Venus have fortunate aspects towards one another, and thus it is not surprising that this May-native feel extremely happy and contented in his married life, in spite of many business troubles and adversities. He writes in a happy mood, as follows: "My wife, born June 12, 1897, half past eleven at night, in the Vogt country, is a *wonderful* wife, who shares with me all good and all evil days."

When there are two good triplicities in the horoscope of happy lovers happily married, indicating good harmony and marital peace, that of course does not keep away the blows of fate, or disturbances coming from without, that is, when other planetary positions, as in the man's horoscope in the 5th house and in the woman's horoscope in the 9th house, are adversely affected by the rays of Saturn or Neptune. But that is a matter for itself, which at this time I do not care to discuss; the chief fact remains that two lovers are so closely attached to one another that they share weal and woe.

In addition to these aspects that are clearly visible there are others, of which I want to refer to a few only, so as not to confuse the layman.

Powers of Stars

In Chart No. 2 we find Mars at a distance of about 75 degrees from Neptune, who does not form an exact aspect; a distance of 72 degrees would be a quintile. Mercury has a distance of about 12 degrees from the Sun, which is more fortunate than if he were too close to the Sun.

All aspects are listed in the ephemeris which are published annually, although not so conveniently grouped. I do hope that every one reading this book carefully will also learn soon to estimate the respective distances of the planets from one another, and to draw his conclusions accordingly.

It is all in the exercise. As soon as the horoscope has been calculated mathematically, it is very easy for one understanding the fundamentals of astrology to tell at first sight whether two planets are in conjunction or in opposition, as one will see in the Charts 4, 9, 14; in the square (90 degrees) as in the Charts Nos. 6 and 21; in the triplicity (120 degrees) as in the Charts Nos. 7 and 8, or in the sextile (60 degrees), as the Sun and Moon stand in Chart No. 5.

As soon as one understands that a horoscope is divided into various divisions or houses, each having its own meaning, and how the aspectarian is set up, one may already have a fair idea about deciphering his own horoscope and that of his affinity, or at least to find out whether it be an easy or a hard lot that one has to bear.

The difficult calculations, and deciphering of many aspects apparently at odds with one another, and not discernible at first sight, these one will learn to know only after many years of intense study. The very best mathematician will not always be cocksure about his opinions (prognosis), since the research material is so large that years are needed before one has correctly understood all explanatory rules. With reference to the assumption that perhaps every one that is educated may estimate a horoscope, it may be well to heed the precept of Joseph August Lux which he formerly published in the "Weissen Heften" (White Pamphlets) : "There is something *not* every one can do, indeed, it is done very seldom. That is, the art of interpretation, for which all textbooks are likely to fail us."

Here, on the field of interpretation, in which we are chiefly interested, one will find all triumphs and all defeats. *Here is located the mystery, the real spirit of the thing, the philosophy, the doctrine concerning the soul and fate, that which is amenable to medicine and cures, or at least a study of character,* a cosmic psychology, but one will also find every possible abuse and nonsense and speculation, as for an exasperating instance in the so-called "astrological bureaus."

Thus no one should believe that, after being able to interpret a few aspects, he will solve all world riddles. As much as we may try to penetrate into the mysteries of the planet powers, many things will remain for us past finding out, and even though we know all astrological laws we shall not be able to discover any one's secrets. With the aid of astrology we may ascertain in the first place what chances there are for a continued living together in love or in friendship, whether or not two characters are well adapted to each other, whether they live at peace according to the chief aspects, or whether to expect much of strife and turmoil on account of severe cross currents.

The best conclusions as to whether two persons will live amiably together, or later become very unhappy, one may draw from the comparison of two horoscopes. For this reason I am giving several examples of horoscopes, in which appear especially the fortunate or unfortunate astral activities.

It may thus be gleaned from various horoscopes whether the soul has a great attractive tendency, whether two persons are drawn to one another through sensual love or through quickly aroused passions, or whether the attachment will transform itself into hatred, loathing, or indifference, and a short happiness in a romantic or in marriage will be followed by a painful separation.

For general purposes one should observe how the orbs of heaven, Sun and Moon stand towards each other in two horoscopes. Permit me to offer another explanation in this regard.

When, for instance, Sun and Moon shed their rays well in triplicity on in Sextile (see Chart No. 9) in the horoscope of the husband, the Moon in Aries; and No. 10, in the horoscope of the wife the Sun in Leo, or No. 7 in Leo and No. 8 in the sign Gemini, or when the Moon in the horoscope of the husband stands where the Sun is in the Horoscope of the wife, or vice versa, there is usually a strong attraction and soul harmony. Both persons feel themselves attached through a strong fluid or through some magnetic radiation. If, however, planets predominate in favor of mind harmony, and Venus and Mars oppose one another, one of the marriage partners remains dissatisfied in sexual intercourse.

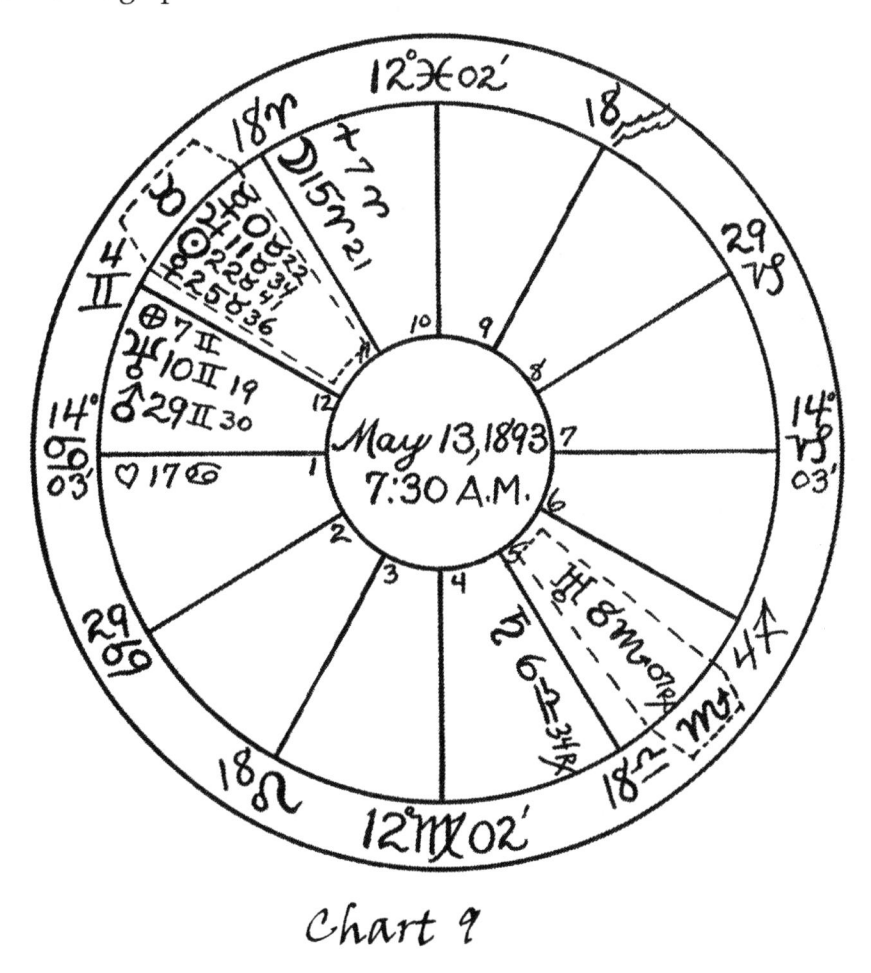

Chart 9

It is, moreover, a known fact that persons whose minds are very highly developed will easily or entirely disappoint in sexual matters, whereas the average persons, who do not absorb their energies of mind as strongly, have a much stronger developed capacity for love, and are more apt to give vent to their temperament.

When in the horoscope of the husband and the wife Sun and Moon stand in quartile or in opposition, and Mars and Venus display their sexual love and passion, the two lovers will find untold difficulties, in spite of deep affection and a strong sensuality, before they may arrive at a pleasant and amiable hour, or even at living together. Despite their erotic affection, as conditioned by Venus and Mars, they will suffer from severe soul conflicts, and never completely understand each other. It is worse when Sun and Jupiter, or Moon, Mars and Jupiter, adversely radiate in two nativities. In such a case there are frequent struggles through differences of opinion, through differences of confession, or opposing views concerning morals, law, and custom, or a disharmony because of external formalities, which are in conflict with their natural desires for love. These are strong soul tangles, as I have depicted them in my volume entitled, "Religion and Love."

Thus when Venus and Mars in the horoscope of two lovers radiate well, and Sun and Moon stand in hostile aspects, or Saturn and Mars offer cross currents, there may be a transient corporeal intercourse, or at times a fleeting emotion for love, nevertheless their emotions will be disturbed, and one of them, who at first sincerely loved and was attached to the other, will have to bear a severe heart affliction through a separation, perhaps both of them. It is truly said by Emanuel Geibel:

> "When two hearts part
> That have dearly loved each other,
> That is a great affliction,
> And there is none greater."

One may not always tell accurately from the Horoscopes of Lovers, whether both are attracted by sexual desire alone, or if their association is of long duration, they will consummate intercourse of a sexual nature, or whether in case of free love, their relationship will develop into marriage sanctioned by law.

In many horoscopes which I have, accordingly, investigated

on the basis of written or personal communications of betrothed or friends, the love and friendship harmony of two persons is well apparent through coinciding aspects of Venus, Mars, and Jupiter (see Charts Nos. 7 and 8), as well as generally speaking, all references to natural desires; it is far more difficult, however, to say whether the authorities and the church will sanction the same. Sun, Moon, Jupiter and Venus usually favor, in good connection, a happy marriage through a marriage by law or church; but if influential planets are hostile, the marriage by law may be annulled after some time. I know of many that were married, both men and women, in whose horoscope Sun and Moon were in conjunction or in triplicity, but who were separated by law after a few years whenever Uranus in one of the horoscopes had a strong afflicting position. (Uranus in the mid-heaven, Chart No. 5, or in the 7th house, (Charts Nos. 14 and 18.) It has been really surprising to me to see that Uranus and Jupiter play an important part in quick marriages and sudden separation. (See horoscope of people that had been married for a short time and had been separated, Charts Nos. 14, 17, and 18.)

In consulting horoscopes of friends and acquaintances living in free love I have observed, and have heard them tell, that they agreed very well with one another when Venus and Mars, or Venus, Sun and Saturn, were in sextile or in triplicity, but also this, that for some reason or other, they never were married legally when in the fundamental horoscopes of those loving and desiring each other Mars and Jupiter were in sharp opposition, when for instance Jupiter or Mars were in Aries in the horoscope of the male, and with the female, Moon or Mars in Cancer, or when Jupiter or Saturn in both horoscopes formed a quartile.

Especially with lovers in whose horoscope Venus and Mercury are in triplicity to Mars, or Moon, of the male or female partner, there is at times a wonderful harmony and affection in personal contact as well as in letters, but suddenly they are sharply at odds through differences of opinion concerning attitudes towards life, or religious or occult problems, when Jupiter somehow has a hostile position towards Mars or Saturn in the nativities of persons that are otherwise at peace.

It is necessary to observe these various activities of planets for many years in the horoscopes of acquaintances and friends, before one may have a clear conception; and, therefore, I shall not ramble too far from the subject. On this subject there is room for many more experiences.

It is said that Mars and Sun, at the same location in the horoscope of lovers, will affect a strong soul attraction and spiritually intensified relations, such as those of Goethe and Frau von Stein.

If, moreover, Venus has its position in the horoscope of the man where Mars is found in the horoscope of a female, or vice versa, when both ostensibly like each other and there are no other hindrances through differences in rank, or through self-mortification or obligation of one part, it will result in a glowing passion, or in a sensuality of short duration. If the one is aesthetically minded, the other would have a need of quietly subduing his inclinations.

If in the horoscope of the man the Moon is in triplicity with Venus, as in Chart No. 7, at a distance of 120 degrees, or a distance of 60 degrees as in Chart No. 11, there exists a strong attraction towards the female sex, and a desire to marry; except in the case that Saturn somehow interferes. (Chart No. 22 in conjunction with Venus and in opposition with Mars.) Whether or not the chances are good for marriage, depends upon the aspects of the planet dominating the 7th house, affecting marriage.

If the 7th house of a horoscope is located under a double bodied sign, such as Pisces, Gemini, or Sagittarius, and Sun and Moon are well radiated in these signs, numerous marriages are likely.

However, this interpretation counts for naught whenever, for instance, the chief planet of the first house Pisces, say, Jupiter and Neptune, contain hostile aspects. Such is the case in the horoscope of a female who hates men, who is born under the double bodied sign of Pisces, as the Sun in the horoscope stands in the double bodied sign of Sagittarius, but the planets dominating the sign Pisces, Neptune and Jupiter, have malific radiation. Jupiter is located in a quartile to Saturn, a fact which in itself is restrictive. The person referred to, since she lost her mother at an early age, was reared in a cloister, and Neptune also has a hostile position towards Venus and the Sun. (See the respective paragraph in Section III, Chart No. 21.)

When the Moon is in the 7th house of a male horoscope, regardless in what sign she is located, this indicates several females, and several marriages, respectively, unless she is adversely radiated by the Sun or Saturn. It is thus necessary to pay close attention to all locations of the planets and their respective aspects, if one would have conclusive evidence, and even then one may err, if not all astrological rules of interpretation referring to love and marriage are known and observed.

One of the ancient astrologists, Claudius Ptolemy, whose rules to this day have proved themselves reliable, stated that, to determine the wife, the position of the Moon in the horoscope of the man is to be considered, as well as its influence. When the Moon is in the eastern quadrant (in consulting a horoscope east is not to the right, as on a map, but to the left, since we have the heaven above us), a person will contract marriage at a very early age, or he will, if he has advanced in years, choose a very young wife.

If the Moon is in the western quadrant, she indicates a later marriage, or that the person influenced by the Moon in the west will wed a worthy and dignified mate. If the Moon still is in conjunction with Saturn in the west, a marriage is denied, and the men stay bachelors; or, if they marry, they will soon become widowers. (Chart No. 6.) There are numerous marriages and love pacts, a fact I often found confirmed, when the Moon is in the double bodied sign of Sagittarius (Chart No. 13), or when the Sun or Jupiter are in triplicity to Uranus (Charts Nos. 15 and 18), favoring rapid legal marriages and rapid divorces as well. Uranus, the planet of surprise, of sudden attraction and alienation, was not yet known by the ancient astrologers, and nothing is noted in earlier works concerning its action. We must, however, take into consideration his influence with regard to love and marriage, because he causes many reforms and changes in this respect.

If in the horoscope of a man Saturn faces the Moon, that indicates a stern, serious, and industrious wife (Chart No. 11), perhaps Capricorn-natures (characters), or women at whose birth the Sun was in Capricorn.

Jupiter, when in favorable aspect to the Moon, indicates active and honorable wives, especially in conducting the household.

Mars is said to offer recalcitrant and pugnacious husbands or wives; the Moon in connection with Venus indicates amiable, agreeable and cheerful characters.

The Moon, faced by Mercury, offers prudent, intelligent mates, with keen expression of character.

A good association of Venus and Jupiter (see Horoscope Charts Nos. 7 and 8), is said to furnish good taste, a marked ability of preparing meals, and a genuine art of living; when Saturn is fortunately combined with Mercury, it will effect harmony in the shaping of one's mode of living, love to the husband and to the children. A conjunction of the Moon with Mars, however, would indicate wives that are given to wrath, inconstant, and fickle. As for a female nativity, the Sun must be regarded as important for the husband. If the latter is in the eastern quartile (as in Chart No. 4), it signifies that those women that are favored by the Sun's radiation will become bethothed at an early period, or, when their youth has faded away, they will be taken into marriage by some youth.

If the Sun is in the western quadrant, it indicates a late betrothal, or bestows a husband in the maturer years.

I have not always found a confirmation of this old rule. When the Sun stood in the 7th house of a female native (Charts Nos. 5 and 10), to my knowledge there was an early betrothal. No. 5 became engaged at 16½ years, and married at 20; No. 10 also married at a tender age, also No. 17. The chief reason for this might be when several planets group themselves about the Sun in a female nativity, for in that case there is no lack of admirers, or when in earlier years there have been important Directions (e.g. Venus in conjunction with the Sun).

Saturn, when somehow connected with the Sun, bequeaths dispassionate, moderate, worthy, and industrious husbands.

Jupiter's gift is an honorable husband, with a great soul.

Mars indicates enterprising, resolute husbands who resist the general ordinances of men, who tolerate neither law nor order.

Venus promises well groomed and handsome husbands.

Mercury bestows men who are good providers, but when the planet is adversely radiated upon by Mars or Saturn, and is retrograde in conjunction with the Sun in the 7th house, it couples with dishonest, false, faithless people, or with criminals. (See Chart No. 17 with description.)

Venus, when connected with Saturn, in the female horoscope, indicates lazy husbands, too feeble for conjugal habits. When Venus is connected with Mars, there are agitated, passionate, and sensual husbands, who break the marriage bond. Most of the men whose horoscopes contain Venus, in conjunction or opposition with Mars, are very sensual and voluptuous. (Charts Nos. 13 and 22.)

Marriage will be solid and permanent, most of the ancient astrologers agree in this, when Sun and Moon in the horoscopes of the lovers radiate each other fortunately (Charts Nos. 7, 8, 9, 10), all the more so when the Moon in the male horoscope and the Sun in the female horoscope face each other in the sextile or triplicity. In the same horoscope, however, counter-rays of other planets may destroy the harmony, when they are radiated upon by progressed planets.

There is danger of divorce and alienation when Sun and Moon are located in a sign not related to them, or in a foreign, or counter-sign, and alternately shed rays; but when the lights of heaven are in related signs, and are mutually connected, and moreover, receive the aspect of a benefic, one may expect a peaceful marriage which is of advantage for both lovers.

Within the aspects of planets threatening disaster, however, one may look for discord, severe temper, and untruthfulness to the detriment of both, and separation. At times it may also happen that between two charts the lights (Sun and Moon) are in unfavorable aspect but the Benifics (Jupiter and Venus) are favorable. Here, the subjects, if married may separate, but forgive one another and begin life together again. The evildoers, by this we mean Saturn and Mars, usually destroy marriage through asperity and meanness. (Charts 14 and 17.) Mercury in its aspect, according to the rules of Ptolemy, is said to carry the news of sordid spots of marriage among the people, and leads to court procedures and the verdict of the judge. The other differences between married people are arrived at from positions of Venus, Mars, and Saturn, by ascertaining whether these planets are in quartile or in opposition to planets in the horoscope of the partner.

If the planets referred to show a good coincidence with Sun and Moon, they determine a legally valid union and a good home, and marriage is conformable to the aspect which Venus takes to one of these planets.

It may happen that Venus is in the position of the Sun of the marriage partner, and at first effects much attraction, but at the same time receives the hostile rays of Saturn in the nativity of the marriage partner, and the mutual affections will soon cool off. In such a case the inner estrangement and coldness of one of the partners may grow into a reason for divorce.

Venus at a good aspect with Saturn is said to indicate an amiable life in marriage, but if Mars interferes, the union cannot be lasting. There will be jealousy and ill will.

If Venus and Saturn are located in signs that are related to themselves or alternately, if for instance Venus is in Capricorn, in the sign of Saturn, or vice versa, Saturn in Libra, the sign of Venus, it is said that may result in a union with blood relations.

Ptolemy says in this regard: If Venus and Saturn are in alternative action on the ascendant (cusp of the first house), or in Medium Coelum (Mid-heaven) (cusp of the 10th house), such a position will indicate that degenerate sons will debauch their mothers or their sisters or their step-mothers; moreover, that immoral women will permit sexual intercourse to their sons, their step-sons, or allow the husband to debauch the daughters. If the Sun is approaching, and the planets stand to the westward, men will debase their daughters or step-daughters. Cases of this kind happen in our days, especially among peasants at remote sections of the country. Such a case of debauchery of our days has been described

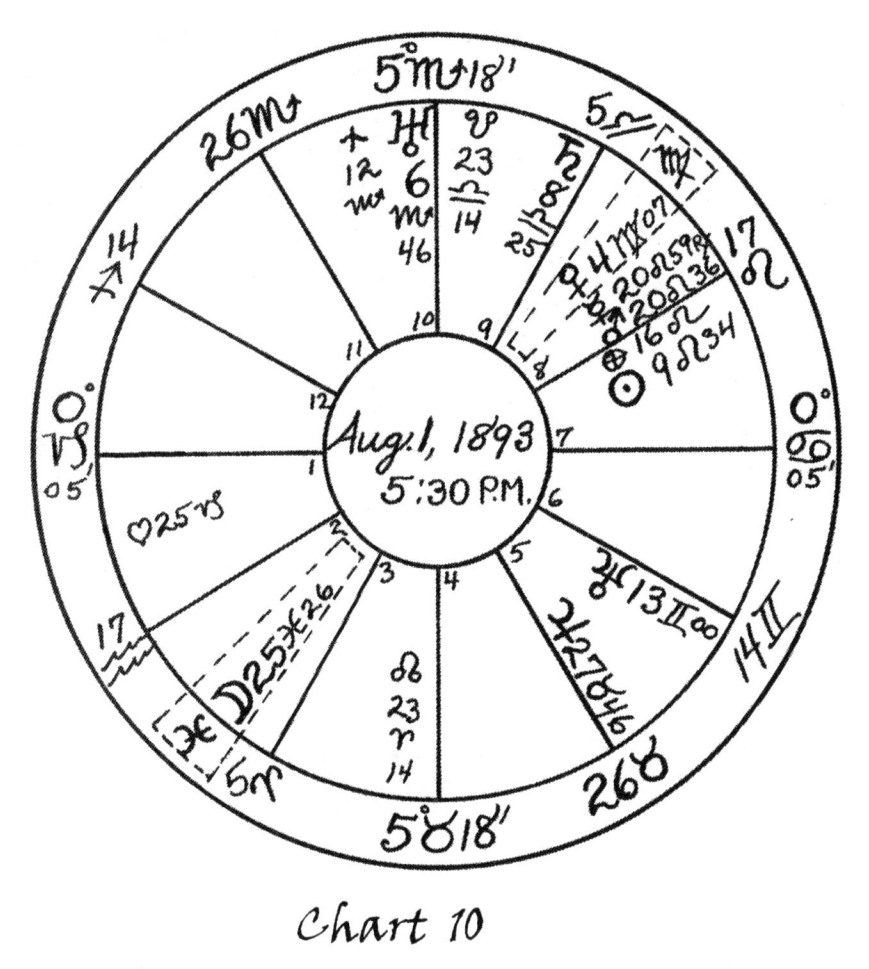

Chart 10

in the book "Lebenslaenglich" (A Life Sentence), "Experiences and Sufferings of Carl Hau," describing a peasant whose wife had died, and who thought it nothing amiss to use his own daughter, until she had conceived, whereupon he was sent to the penitentiary.

Generally speaking, Mars designates the kind of sexual

inclinations of men. If that planet is separated from Venus and Saturn, in the aspect of Jupiter, it produces men who live decently in marriage, preserving the faith, and do not ask for any unnatural sexual habits. If connected with Saturn only, Mars will render phlegmatic, a rather cool union; in conjunction with Venus and Jupiter, however, and mutually joined through some aspect,

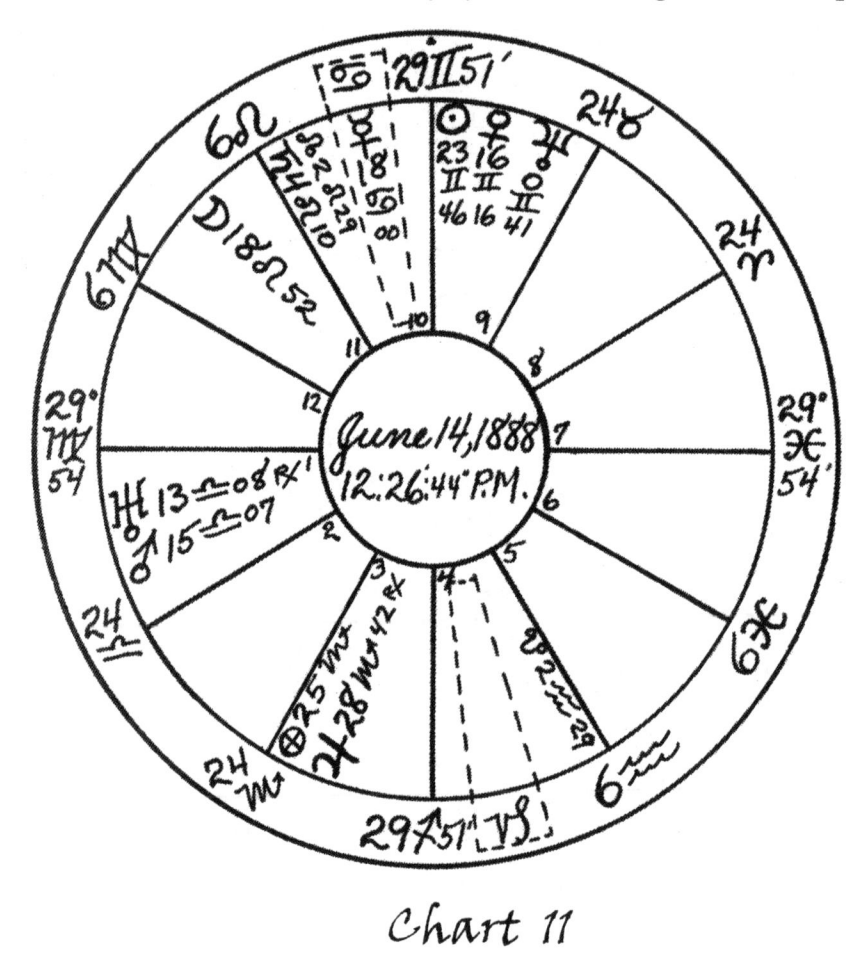

Chart 11

Mars will bequeath a disposition ready for, and asking for, love; nevertheless the lover is contented and always intent upon avoiding ugly manners and a bad reputation.

When Mars stands alone with Venus, or when Jupiter and retrograde Saturn is also present, husbands are voluptuous, using every opportunity to satisfy their desires. Whenever one of the two planets is in position in the evening, the other in the morning (Venus is a morning star), this causes an inclination to gratify one's lust for the male and female alike, so that on both sides they over indulge. (This means people inclined to be bi-sexual). When both planets are in an evening position they indicate a burning desire for contact with *women* only. If, on the other hand, both planets, Venus and Mars, are

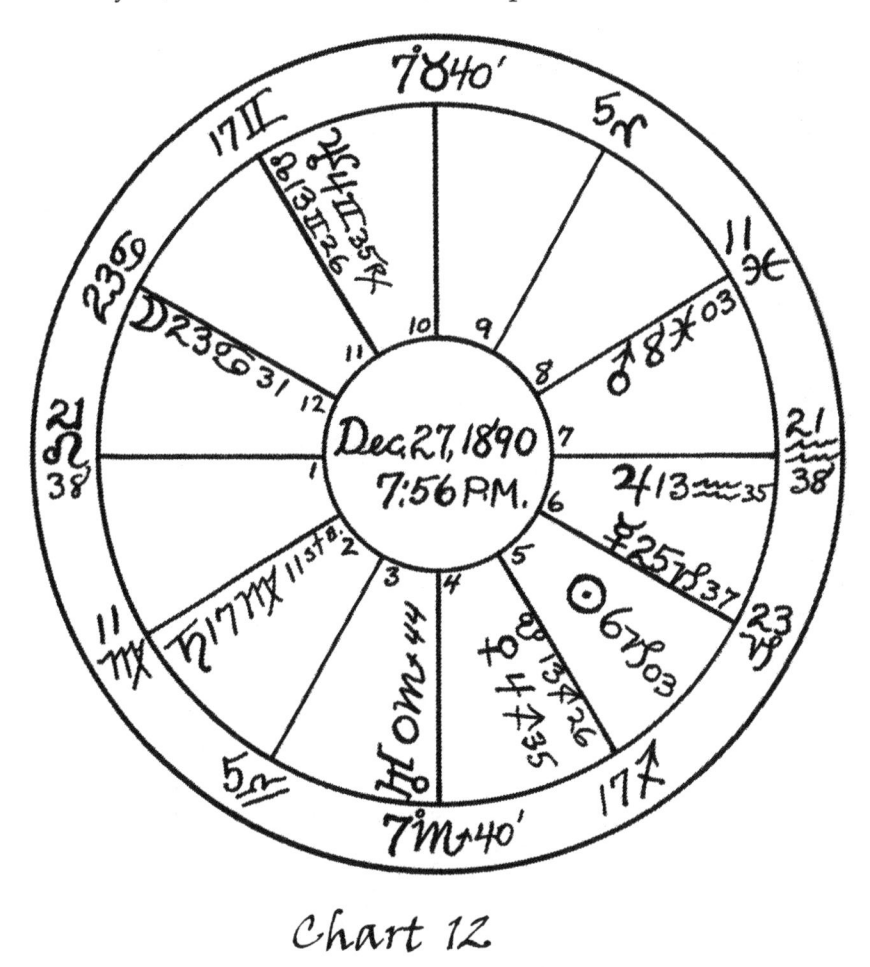

Chart 12

located in the morning, those that are influenced are caught with a desire to contact with men.

If Venus stands to the east in the horoscope, men will deal with loose women, with servants, or strangers; if Mars has that position in the east (Chart No. 3), men will associate with women of a higher standing, or with their landladies.

As for the romances of women, the position occupied by Venus in their horoscopes must be considered. If Venus is in a sign with Jupiter and Mercury, it will make for a moderate and cultivated intercourse. If Venus is connected with Mercury only, without Jupiter, it will, according to Ptolemy, make prone to love and sexual intercourse, but these will be women that abide by the truth, with a mind largely discreet, and fleeing vice. There is a great work of M. Pegius, entitled, "A Book of Nativity Hours," edited by Otto Wilhelm Barth, of Munich. In the same it is noted that Venus and Mercury, when connected, will bestow a love for the arts, poetry, music, dancing, and an amiable and reasonable disposition. This, then, refers to women who enjoy love with reason, and who do not recklessly abandon themselves. Sentiment and reason complement each other.

If Venus, in a female horoscope, stands alone with Mars, or in the same aspect, it will produce cheap and lascivious women, who are also indolent. The same is the case when Jupiter is added. If Mars is covered by the rays of the Sun, these women will seduce servants, or they have illicit connection with abject men or strangers.

Venus, when sunk in the rays of the Sun (e.g. in close conjunction), makes women the mistresses of those of a higher rank, or of the landlords. If Sun and Venus stand in opposition to Neptune, here will rather be aversion against sexual action. (Chart No. 21.) If the signs, and consequently the planets, are feminine, they delight in receiving their passion; if, however, the planets are masculine, through the influence of their position, they indicate people who entice others to love and seduce them. When Saturn is thus connected by aspect with planets, and even in a feminine position, it is the originator of vice. If the planet stands to the east, it will lead to groveling love and make one of ill repute in an extraordinary manner. Jupiter on the contrary, will soften such dispositions, and temper them. These general rules may suffice to inform one to some extent regarding the problems of love and of marriage. Whoever will take the trouble of carefully checking back a large number of nativities of lovers on the basis of these rules, will soon understand what great power the stars will exert upon us, and that our fate is anchored above; and he will also know that all hoping and love's longing is in vain, unless the fulfillment of the most ardent wishes *is written in the stars*.

Advantages and Disadvantages in the Character of Lovers

Let him prove himself whoever assumes eternal ties.
-Schiller.

Although according to natural laws lovers feel a strong attachment to each other, and much rather would want to think and believe only the best of each other, huge deceptions will nevertheless appear; for, as we all know, love is blind.

Accordingly, it is of value for every one to be in the position to inform himself, at least to some extent, about the advantages and disadvantages of the person adored. Certainly astrology is a very good aid for this purpose.

Even for one who fails to penetrate into all details of astrological science, or to compare the aspects of one's own horoscope, as explained in the previous chapter, with the charts of those near to him, it will be of some benefit to know of the influences which the Sun bestows upon the natives as they are born in their respective months.

As for the fundamental influence for the character and the fortunes of a person, astrological doctrine ascribes that to the sign rising at the moment of birth on the eastern horizon: the *ascendant*. This must, however, be first calculated according to the exact time of birth.

The charts in this volume, which completely deviate from one another, show which diversified signs arise in the same month, and what peculiar figures of heaven are formed by the moving of the stars. One may easily ascertain the chief characteristics of a person, when the birthday is known as well as the position of the Sun in the horoscope, since the Sun stands annually in the same sign on the same day.

Judged by the influence of the Sun, the general dispositions of character of males as well as of females are quite positive for those having their birthday between March 21 and April 20, since the Sun in Aries bestows upon men and women a vivacious temperament, much ambition, zeal, initiative, impulsiveness, the quality to enthuse others, confidence in one's self, courage, boldness, intrepidity, but this also includes irritability, a hot and explosive temper, a tendency to act prematurely, so that those who are influenced by Aries will have to ascribe to themselves the weal and woe of their lives. Most of those who are dominated by Aries are also somewhat tyrannical, vehement and refractory, and many a person does not know what he wants, he is as changeable as the weather, as April is.

As I am emphasizing in my annuals, published every year, "A Vision of the Future," I must do the same here, that for the disposition of character the sign in which the Sun stands is never final, but that the sign rising in the east in the hour of birth should also be recognized. (For instance, Aquarius in Chart No. 3.) If, however, at the birth of a person having his birthday between March 20th and April 20th, the negative sign of Cancer, the house of the Moon, arises in the hour of birth, there often exists in addition to the qualities bestowed by the sign Aries, a moral flimsiness, especially when combinations of Venus, Moon and Neptune correspond with Mars, Uranus and Saturn in the horoscope. In itself the sign of Cancer is a chief or cardinal sign; its influence may be positive, according to the aspects still cooperating. At any rate the combination referred to reveals much of a tendency to dominate and usually some ascendancy in life, when the Sun is in Aries in the 10th and 11th house of the horoscope. When there are characteristics leading to success in life, these of course do not exclude moral weakness or a weak romance. A man whose horoscope shows the Sun in Aries may, for instance, be gifted artistically, he may even be a genius in his sphere of activity, in his office or calling, but is known as an overbearing personality, although he may be a weakling in the presence of a woman, in the event he is overruled by his sentiments. The love spells and impulsive notions of the Aries-people, of course, are not too insistent, and reason will again resume its rightful place, or they look for other pastime. The prevailing influences of the stars would have to be especially good, if the love of an Aries-character is to be enduring, and married life to be permanently happy.

The general dispositions of people having their birthday between April 21st and May 21st, in whose horoscopes the Sun in Taurus exerts his influence, naturally show a great longing for love and attachment, a propensity for gayety and companionship, a great predilection for music and an interest in art, but also an inclination to believe in dreams, and an interest in occult sciences. They often feel a strong attraction towards the opposite sex, to people at whose birth the Sun was in Scorpio, but in consequence are at times greatly disappointed. Many born at the end of April or in first part of May suffered disappointments and sad events during the last years up to 1926 from the influence of Saturn, who stood for many months in opposition to their Sun location. With the clearing of the skies relief in various forms should have been felt, especially for those born in May, of the younger generation who experienced their first love, the years 1928 to 1932 were very promising, and even more enjoyable also for the older set.

Those who are influenced by the sign of Taurus are very tenacious and enduring in their work and in forging ahead, but also full of inflexible stubbornness. They know what they want and they carry it through, nor will they be easily downed by fate or be hampered in their plans and enterprises. Usually they have a great deal of patience; they are able to hide or suppress their feelings for a long time, but when they are provoked for any reason, and their patience is at an end, they may be severe, explosive, and wrathful, although they are otherwise even tempered. (Charts Nos. 5, 7 and 9.)

The general disposition of people having their birthdays

between May 21st, May 22nd, respectively, and June 21st, at whose birth the Sun was in the lofty sign of Gemini in the house of Mercury, do not take life too tragic, except certain planet activities are predominating which depress them. They have diversified talents and, according to known astrological rules, are dual natures, their word rather differing from their action. They are of a versatile character, a mixture of lofty intellectual faculties and doubt, and they are likely to dissipate. They know how to adapt themselves generally in all circumstances, and they often have many irons in the fire. It is not surprising that their romance would be rather turbulent, so that they will find themselves in great agony of soul, and also have their secrets. For men and women as well, born in June, the years 1927 to 1929 was indicated to be quite dreary, while Saturn in the sign of Sagittarius sent his hostile rays to the sign Gemini. Unless there were counter currents at the position of stars in their fundamental horoscope, their otherwise sanguine character was subjected to be somewhat dejected. At the middle of 1929 a happier period produced a change for those who weathered the critical season, and that period perpetuated itself into 1930. When Jupiter is near the Sun for those who are influenced by the sign of Gemini, that means good prospects for their romance and friendly relations. (The Sun stands in the sign Gemini in the Charts Nos. 8 and 11.)

The general dispositions of people having a birthday between June 22nd and July 23rd, who are influenced by the sign Cancer, the heaven house of the Moon, will be subject to great vacillation of sentiment in their emotions, and they will be rather inconstant. Their faculty for a family is marked; they have a great longing for a cozy home, but they are not easily at rest, except certain changes take place in their fortunes, such as journeys, a change of scenes. The men that are influenced by Cancer often are too sensitive, their sense of honor is easily violated. They attribute a great meaning to external appearances. Most of those influenced by Cancer are inclined to polygamy, and they keep company with several at the same time, and have several romances. It depends upon the position of the individual planet, especially upon Mercury and Uranus, whether or not their moral aberrations remain secret, or whether there will be an open scandal. Cancer characters are easily led, to the good as well as to the evil, and it depends upon the society they keep, and whether they are boosted or dragged down by the wild waves of life. Many Cancer characters have a motherly instinct, they are home people and provide for the home, as soon as they have made proper connection. Some are timid and backward, they change their minds, they are not trustworthy, so that it is best no longer to rely on their promises.

Those born between July 1st and 11th are said to have kindness -- in spite of many weaknesses of character, and their quest for great things. Thus there are highly genial people found among the Cancer types, such as adventurers and criminals, such as settle down and others that lead the life of a nomad. Most of those influenced by the Sun in Cancer travel about the world. Between the years 1927 to 1929 those born at the end of June likely lead a turbulent life; between 1930 and 1934 those born in July also, and it is rather probable that they met with painful losses, they will have their difficulties with the authorities, with courts, trials, sharp altercations with their enemies. The women likewise, as they are dominated by the sign Cancer, were much agitated, but chiefly through the fortunes of their husbands. (See Charts Nos. 14 and 17, with the Sun in Cancer.)

Speaking of characteristic traits in general of people born between July 24th and August 23rd, under the influence of the Sun in the royal sign Leo, the sign of the Sun, these have a strong power of resistance against the battles of life, they are proud of character, benign and noble. If however, the radiation of the Sun is less fortunate, these traits may degenerate into vain gloriousness and bragging, boastfulness, exaggerations, self-adulation and exaltation. These people usually crave for apparent wealth, splendor, glory, they often are extremely ambitious and seek honors. Of course, it also depends upon the sign arising in the east at the hour of birth to tell, whether one's activity in public will be as hoped for in the case of those that are mostly influenced by Leo.

It is quite remarkable that many persons that have been prominent in the history of the world have been influenced by the Sun in Leo, such as Frederick the Great, Napoleon I., a large number of politicians, some of whom suddenly ascended to great heights, but just as sudden have fallen.

A proof in point is the lot of Emperor Charles I. of Austria-Hungary, who, fell rapidly after the last lofty ascent he dared, and who ended a life that had been begun in splendor, upon a lonely isle.

Persons born in August, during the years 1914 to 1918, whose location of the Sun in Leo have their Sun adversely aspected by Uranus in Aquarius, will at some later period have a less happy romance than those born in August in other years. Many of the persons referred to will suffer much affliction through relatives in their 19th or 20th year, or they will experience the woe and suffering of love, and later know of sudden attachments and alienations, with much sorrowful longing and separation. Generally speaking those who are influenced by the Sun in Leo during the years 1927 to 1929 will see much of good things or some favorable change, according to aspects that are still active.

People born between August 24th and September 23rd, as the Sun is in the sign of Virgo, in the house of Mercury, are rather prudent and intelligent; they have business ability or scientific interests, a faculty to discern matters and to criticise sharply. Some have nagging tendencies, so that they often meddle into other people's affairs and lose their sympathies. Very many people that are influenced by the sign of Virgo at times have not enough confidence in themselves, they are likely to doubt and droop their heads, as the Sun stands to the east or west at their birth, they are either adapted for some higher office, a position of confidence, or for some subordinate position.

As husbands those born in the sign of Virgo are good providers, they are always intent upon the good of their family and of all those endeared to them, especially when they have found a good mate. However, they concern themselves in married life about every small item. They are rather narrow-minded and want an account given of the smallest expense. For this reason parsimonious housewives are more suitable for those that care only for their own home, than women accustomed to do big things and have many interests. Of those who are dominated by the Sun in the sign of Virgo, even when a greater field of public activity is assigned to them, it will always be said, "My home is my world." Ordinarily their place is rather in subordinated positions. Only when the Sun at their birth was in Zenith, or when influential planets are well radiated, they have a chance to become directors of major corporations, or to assume a higher public office. In most cases theirs will be a rough sea to travel.

Reason will rather assert itself in their love affairs, whereas their sentiments will sometimes appear on the surface. If there is always order and punctuality at home, and people always respect their interests, they are satisfied.

People who are born between September 24th and October 23rd, and in whose horoscope the Sun is in the sign of Libra, the second house of Venus, are reputed generally to have a propensity for equalizing justice, and a noble character. They are polite, friendly, pleasing, amiable, they know how to adapt themselves in all given circumstances; they also show a predilection for music and song, artistic productions, sociability. Their happiness in love and marriage will fluctuate. Much depends with those influenced by Libra upon the partner chosen to make a peaceful and harmonious union. People born amidst good aspects, strive for the ideal, but they usually lack in will power and perseverance. When there are oppositions of several planets in the horoscope of lovers, some of which are strongly influenced by Libra, there are severe altercations; however, a compromise is possible if but one of the partners is reasonable and knows how to keep silence at the right moment.

Of a man born October 3rd, 1880, in whose horoscope Sun, Moon, Mars, Mercury stood in Libra, with Mars in opposition to Jupiter, and Mercury in opposition to Saturn, one of his divorced wives tells me that up to date, in 1923, he had been married three times, and that he was again divorced, and forthwith had another love affair. Yet he was doing his best to support every one of his wives or at least make some provision for them. That is surely a strange case. Love and marriage usually play an important part with those who are influenced by the sign Libra, and they are often beset by very peculiar complications

There may be married Libra people, nevertheless, living a quiet and peaceable life, when they are well mated.

The chief characteristics of people born between October 24th and November 22nd, in whose horoscope the Sun is in conjunction with several planets in the sign of Scorpio in the house of Mars (see Charts Nos. 18 and 19), are their ardent passions which easily may lead to extremes. As a rule they are very erotic, and possess much will power. The Sun in Scorpio bestows upon those born under this influence great sensitiveness and magnetism; accordingly they easily attract others and make many friends. They have a great deal of self-respect, and they are very receptive for praise and recognition. In all their endeavors they display much energy, no matter what object they have in view. Many have a burning desire for worldly power, others strive after nobler, intellectual objects; they search through all problems of life, and they are always on the research. Others again show a special liking for secret objects, for mysticism and occult sciences, others again abandon themselves entirely to base instincts, until they arrive at a better knowledge. Accordingly we find among those influenced by the Sun in Scorpio higher and baser types in sharp contrast, beginning from the highbrow scientists, the genial poets and thinkers, down to the adventurer, the moron, and the murderer, as I have already explained at length in the last annuals for 1925 and 1926. (*e.g.* horoscope of Friedrich Haarmann, who committed wholesale murder, Annual for 1925, p. 125.)

Among the families of those influenced by Scorpio, especially when Mars and Saturn in their horoscope exchange hostile rays, tragic events will be recorded, the sudden or violent death of relatives. Female Scorpio-types having great intellectual aspirations usually entertain high expectations concerning their husbands; an ordinary average human being would hardly suffice. They want to be stimulated, and they always look for something new, especially when in sexual matters they are not satisfied.

Whenever females that are influenced by Scorpio do not find any one to understand their individual disposition, or when they cannot look up to their husbands with complete respect, they feel a profound vacuum in their lives, and they are in quest for people with higher accomplishments, in order to find something for stimulation and pastime.

Many men and women, that are influenced by Scorpio, either through the rising or the Sun-sign, and at whose birth Neptune, Uranus, or Saturn stood in the 7th house of their horoscope, may expect great disappointments in their love affairs or in marriage -- always in the years when Saturn passes through the sign Scorpio, as in 1926, or through the sign of Taurus, as in the years 1940 to May of 1942. Amidst such influence of Saturn they are subject to grave personal conflicts, and the younger generations are affected with all those strokes of fortune or woes in love affairs which I have described at length in my annual for 1926 in the chapter "Taurus" (for May-types), and "Scorpio" for November-types. Men who are influenced by Scorpio, and women as well, at times have their severe private struggles, even from their very youth -- see sketch of character of the native born November 3, 1904, No. 18, and the peculiar type born November 4, 1895, No. 19.

According to ancient astrological experiences the first third of the life of those influenced by Scorpio, or even the first half, is said to be a hard battle. Not before they are settled in their own minds, when they have made headway by hard labor, and they arrive at some quietude, and their chances are evening up, will their life be more peaceful and more harmonious; with most of them this will take place in the middle of the thirties and after severe reverses.

As for special events the planet activities under important directions are decisive, although these usually come under Transits (planet passages). When the aspects are rather fortunate, life is made easy, disharmonious aspects render it difficult.

The general dispositions of males and females having their birthdays between November 23rd and December 22nd, in whose horoscope the Sun is in the sign Sagittarius, in the house of Jupiter, are as follows: A vivid phantasy, frankness, courage, boldness, impulsiveness, vivaciousness of the native, unless a negative sign, as for instance Pisces stands in the east (see Chart No. 21), this lowers the vivaciousness and tends to make melancholy -

- moreover a good heart, a willingness to help, a strong notion of and great desire for independence, some daring at times, and a certain stubbornness of character. Many of those influenced by the sign of Sagittarius are very easily aroused to enthusiasm, to idealism, and vagaries; they are also inclined towards sports and show a predilection for being outdoors, for games requiring plenty of movement, and for travel.

The baser Sagittarius-types, though they are really goodhearted, are easily incensed, and hotheaded of character, being usually sorry for it later. They like to be contrary and take the opposite side. Their wrath is rarely of long duration; nevertheless they waste a great deal of energy through their excitability. In general the Sagittarius-types act as their heart dictates, according to their sentiments and intuitive knowledge rather than according to sober and critical judgment, especially when Mercury, also in the sign of Sagittarius, is not far from the Sun. The Sun, when in the sign of Sagittarius, generally bestows upon those born under his influence much vital stamina and ardent expectations, so that these types will more readily pass off the moody aspects of life (see Chart No. 20, and description of same). Only in case where there are many unfavorable planet influences prevailing in a fundamental horoscope, as in Chart No. 21, will health and resistance be weakened. Otherwise the rule holds good for most of those born at the end of November to December 22nd, as expressed in the words of the humorist, Julius Stettenheim: "This is the true science of living, not to become old, but well along in years." The heart of most of those influenced by Sagittarius remains young forever, and many marry not only once but several times in life, in spite of numerous disappointments and ill fortune. This will also be shown in examples. See Chart No. 20, together with the written confession of a female still ready to marry, regardless of sad experiences with males.

Not all of those influenced by the Sun in Sagittarius, of course, marry several times, but they have no lack of love and adoration, nor of opportunities for several unions. With some the desire of being free and independent is so strongly developed as to rather indulge in free love after adverse experiences, or they forego new love affairs rather than be obligated by law a second or third time. Sometimes the relatives must be considered. At any rate it is less frequent that those influenced by the Sun in Sagittarius do not marry unless some abnormality is involved, or the respective person has a peculiar aversion or fear of marriage, such as the female born November 24th, 1886, who shuns every contact with men. Her biography is contained in the third chapter of this volume. (Chart No. 21.)

The chief traits of people having birthdays between December 23rd and January 20th, at whose birth the Sun stood in the sign of Capricorn, have a natural ambition to make headway in life, and they distinguish themselves by great industry and a tenacious vigor. They usually have much patience, perseverance and persistency in all they undertake. They are quite frugal and inclined to be economical. While the men that are influenced by the sign of Capricorn show a strong interest in politics, the women are noted for practical pursuits; they are good housewives and take things as they are. (See Chart No. 12).

The fundamental trait of those influenced by Capricorn is a solemn mind. They do not waste their time, but seek to improve upon every hour to attain the goal they are striving for. In so doing they consider all things from a practical and economical point of view, especially when the Moon also or some influential planet near the Sun is in Capricorn. Sometimes those that are influenced by Capricorn are moody, taciturn, diffident, and likely to be melancholy; for this reason they should be supplied with a sunny and happy type for their affections as well as married life. Persons born in May or in September would in general fare well with those born in January; however, one should also consider how the planets otherwise radiate each other in the horoscope of lovers. At times the Capricorn types are obstinate and violent, so that the harmony, or disharmony, of marriage depends upon the degree in which life partners will control themselves when altercations are about to come, whether they pout for a long time, or soon make up. Many that are born in Capricorn like to be alone, they remain indifferent and inaccessive, and sometimes marriage is frustrated when Saturn is not favorable. Those that are influenced by Capricorn rarely marry at an early age, except there are special signs to indicate this in their horoscopes. When Capricorn rises in the east, placing the 7th house under Cancer, it is rather likely, at good aspects, that there are two marriages.

The special traits of people having a birthday between January 21st and February 19th, in whose horoscope the Sun is in Aquarius in the house of Uranus, are originality, an intuition for the practical discernment of character, and occult sciences. In general they are philanthropic, benign, tolerant, and have a liberal attitude of life, which is modified only when several planets or the Moon are in Capricorn. The higher Aquarius types are idealistic, noble characters, upright and sympathetic, very faithful in pacts of friendship when once entered upon, even though their life is subject to vicissitudes. Because of their peculiar disposition and altruistic habit of thought they are not understood by many and are regarded as odd. It is an astrological fact that almost all people, at whose birth the Sun stood in Aquarius, once in their life arrive at an extraordinarily critical situation, that they lose their wealth or their belongings, or otherwise have very ill fortune. When radiated unfortunately the sign of Aquarius is very confusing and chaotic. Some people that are influenced by Aquarius are friendly, but also wily, sly, and have many secrets in their personal affairs. They may at times have ill success, but they often emerge from heavy defeats. In their love affairs they are less faithful and positive as in their pacts of friendship; they are subject to many changes, according to the respective aspects of their planets, since their actions may attract as well as repel, and since they incline to romance.

Many Aquarius types also have highly intellectual propensities; they have a multiplicity of interests or an inventive mind. Their sentiments vacillate, they seem to be capricious and freakish at times. They will see things in a roseate light, then again they suddenly become gloomy and lost in thoughts.

People at whose birth the Sun is in the sign of Pisces in the house of Neptune, that is, who are born between February 19th and March 20th, are of a lovelorn type, they are very goodhearted, capable of sympathy and pity for all that are in need of help. They are easily irritated, easily influenced, they bubble over with sentiment, and are melancholic. Most of those influenced by the sign Pisces are easily irritated and insulted, they feel themselves neglected, and they often have to contend with great failures and bitter disappointments, in their affections as well as in friendly relations. At times they feel as though the whole world has conspired against them. They often take certain things too tragically, when others easily rise above them. A chief trait of those that somehow are influenced by the sign Pisces, be that by the Sun in this sign, or when the sign in their horoscope rises in the east, is their great predilection for animals.

They have sympathy for all suffering creatures, and they like to attend to their wants. For those who are influenced by the sign Pisces one may expect personal happiness only moderately, they are confronted everywhere with obstacles and hindrances, neither would their romance or their married life be spared. Rarely will they be exultant beyond measure. Most of those influenced by the sign of Pisces are softhearted, tolerant, and sometimes subject to the will of a stronger type. Thus there is danger for these people of being selfishly exploited by others, because of their yielding disposition, their desire to do justice to everyone. If those that are influenced by the sign of Pisces would not have a capacity for all that is noble and true, and if they would not mean well, they would, with a preponderance of critical factors, be haplessly snatched away by the maelstrom of life, and degenerate into moral baseness. When those who are influenced by the sign of Pisces are favored with fortunate rays of the heaven lights (Sun in triplicity or sextile to the Moon), their noble and beneficent disposition will prove to be their own protection, so that they do not easily fall a prey to every temptation, as those would who are less favorably influenced, nor would they err from the way.

The influence of the sign Pisces bestows a propensity for mysticism, occultism and religiosity, usually with a certain tinge of the romantic. Nevertheless, they will in all things prove themselves rather inconstant, because they react too easily to all external influences, so that their attitudes and views change in the course of life.

If there are several negative influences in the horoscope of those that are influenced by the sign of Pisces, or if for instance the Moon is in conjunction with Neptune, a discerning faculty (aptitude for the study of medicine) is present.

Many men, as well as women, that are born between the end of February and March 20th, will often be dissatisfied with themselves and strike a pessimistic mood. For this reason their character is hard to understand, they will be misunderstood and bitterly disappointed by those whom they like, and in whom they have boundless confidence. Very seldom those that are influenced by the sign of Pisces feel the urge to seek a public office. They will be conspicuous only when the Sun stands in the 9th or 10th house of their horoscope, and in such a case they are usually driven by fate to assume some public office. By dint of their own energy they attain lofty positions, honors and achievements, but they must overcome extreme difficulties and enmities, since the influence of the sign of Pisces will bestow great fortune only in exceptional cases.

Most people, men as well as women, at whose birth the Sun is in the sign of Pisces, have opportunity to marry repeatedly, especially when there are other indications. When unfavorable planetary aspects spoil the influence of the Sun, or when negative influences prevail, we shall, of course, find also weak men among all types, as they are best characterized by Mantegazza in the following:

"The weak husband is a human being of indefinite sex, the body being virile, and the soul feminine. We do find, by the way, especially in our times, many women with a masculine spirit (see the last chapter, the Author), one of the many aberrations committed by nature, when it displaces the proper place of things, a printer's devil for which there is no adequate correction.

The weak husband perhaps has a lusty fist and a strong spirit, but when he is called upon to use these two forces, they do not respond upon the call, and they mock him.

Nothing is more despicable in the eyes of women that a weak man. They will pardon physical debility, but never that of the soul.

Character of Lovers

The truth of this is emphasized by the fact that the most warlike brigands always will have impassionate sweethearts, the geniuses among men, even those of advanced age, will always have affectionate wives, but cowards and men who falter always have been detested and pitied.

And this is quite proper: the laws of nature must be respected, and no one may violate them with impunity.

When the parts are exchanged in marriage, and the wife is stronger than the husband, she will utilize him as a handy instrument which may be used for anything, but down in her heart she pities and detests him, and in the mean time she will look beyond her husband towards that man to whom she can give body and soul, of whose love she may be inordinately proud.

The wife that is superior feels herself humbled because the husband stands lower than she does, and she treats him at best much as one would treat children, pitifully, with all regard, like some being requiring protection and toleration."

That Mantegazza has given a concise and keen description of the psychology of love, is borne out by some confessions of women that were dissatisfied and wanting and longing for a new love, referred to in the last chapter of this volume: "Fortunes and Love Tragedies"

The subsequent remarks of Mantegazza, similar to those of Dr. Weininger, are just as correct as the preceding:

"When the wife lies in the arms of her husband whom she loves, she wants to look up to meet his eyes, and she would want to be on tiptoes to kiss him. God has made her of smaller stature than us, so that she may look up from below. Her eyes will then become more beautiful, the lips part like the chalice of a flower which drinks the dewdrops from on high, and happily and proudly she ejaculates, 'How tall you are!'

If it is for her, however, to cast her eyes downward, they will become small, the proud eyes seem to be transformed into shameful ones; they tell of protection, not admiration, perhaps tenderness, but never pride, and if she does not say, 'Oh, how small you are!' it is because she is good and conceals the pity, not to make still smaller the one she loves.

But even though she does not say it, she thinks so just the same, and this idea sours the best aspirations of feminine ideals, of that almighty enthusiasm, a pair of loving joys."

Permit me also to clearly explain the influence of the Moon, similar to that of the Sun, in the respective signs of the Zodiac, so that every one may draw his conclusions.

Men, as well as women, at whose birth the *Moon stands in the sign of Aries,* in the house of Mars, (Chart No. 14), are by nature of an impulsive and vivacious temper, they have strong and ardent desires, a strong appetite in satisfying their sex appeal, unless Saturn weakens that influence (Chart No. 9). They are capable of great enthusiasm and sexual exaltation in their affections, and they are easily incensed, but the original fire of their enthusiasm may be extinguished just as fast, and they give their attention or their sympathy to some other male or female, especially when they think their kind is not understood. Whenever those who are influenced by Aries cannot live their life, nor have a suitable partner in marriage, with whom they find a response to their superabundant affections, they easily become irritated, violent, impatient, excited, nervous, and quarrelsome. Under certain circumstances they are just as likely to be reconciled again, that is, when they can have their own way about it. This is also the case when in addition to the Moon, or without the same, Mars stands in Aries, for in this sign it is in its own element and encourages to greater sprightliness, to energy, action, and to overcome all obstacles. The Moon or influential planets in Aries enhance vigor and bestow optimism and initiative. Those influenced by the Moon in Aries, to be sure, at times act prematurely and in haste, so that they in consequence rue many a step they have not properly considered, especially when they have married too soon. (See Chart No. 9.)

When opposite currents are strong, it is not out of the

question that persons much attached to each other will separate suddenly, that engagements or marriages will be dissolved. (See for inst. Moon in Aries at the first cusp of the horoscope of a divorced woman (born July 21, 1886, 10 P.M., at Leipzig -- Chart No. 14).

Here the Moon stands sharply in opposition to Jupiter 0 degree, 51 minutes Libra, to Uranus 4 degrees, 19 minutes Libra, and in Platic aspect to Mars in the 7th house. It is not surprising that in the married life of this woman, regardless of the interference of the mother-in-law, (Moon's South Node in the 12th house) there should be differences of opinion, spitefulness, and strife daily, and that the union was dissolved, since the Moon exerted its influence in Aries in opposition to three powerful planets such as Jupiter, Uranus and Mars. Compare also the planet constellation with the planets of the divorced husband (Chart No. 13), of January 20th, 1887, 6:45 P.M., and it will be apparent that in both horoscopes the signs of the Sun oppose one another, that Uranus and Mars in both horoscopes are located almost on the same place, in the male horoscope Uranus 12 degrees Libra, in female Mars 11 degrees Libra; also that the Node of the Moon, rising and descending (the latter in the 7th house of the nativity) of the husband is at quartile to Neptune in her and his horoscope, also that Saturn and Mars in both horoscopes adversely radiate each other, etc.

If in the horoscope of women the Moon is in Aries, they do not tolerate any supervision, they would rather want to dominate themselves, and are very selfwilled. They are likely to develop into house tyrants, when they are not conscious of some strong authority; a husband that is weakly and yielding (as Mantegazza describes him on previous pages), may easily become a henpeck at her presence. With women influenced by the Moon in Aries their reasoning powers, aside of acting upon the impulse, is much developed.

When the Moon in Aries is adversely radiated upon by Saturn, as in the horoscope of a husband, born May 13, 1893, No. 9, the traits already referred to are present, he may become easily enraged or highly enthused, but may cool off and sober down to an extent that appears to be cruel. People at whose birth the Moon stood in

Aries, will in general best agree with those at whose birth the Sun or several planets stood in the fiery sign of Leo or Sagittarius, or in the sign of Aquarius or Gemini; however, it is best to investigate whether or not opposing currents of influential planets might destroy the good harmony.

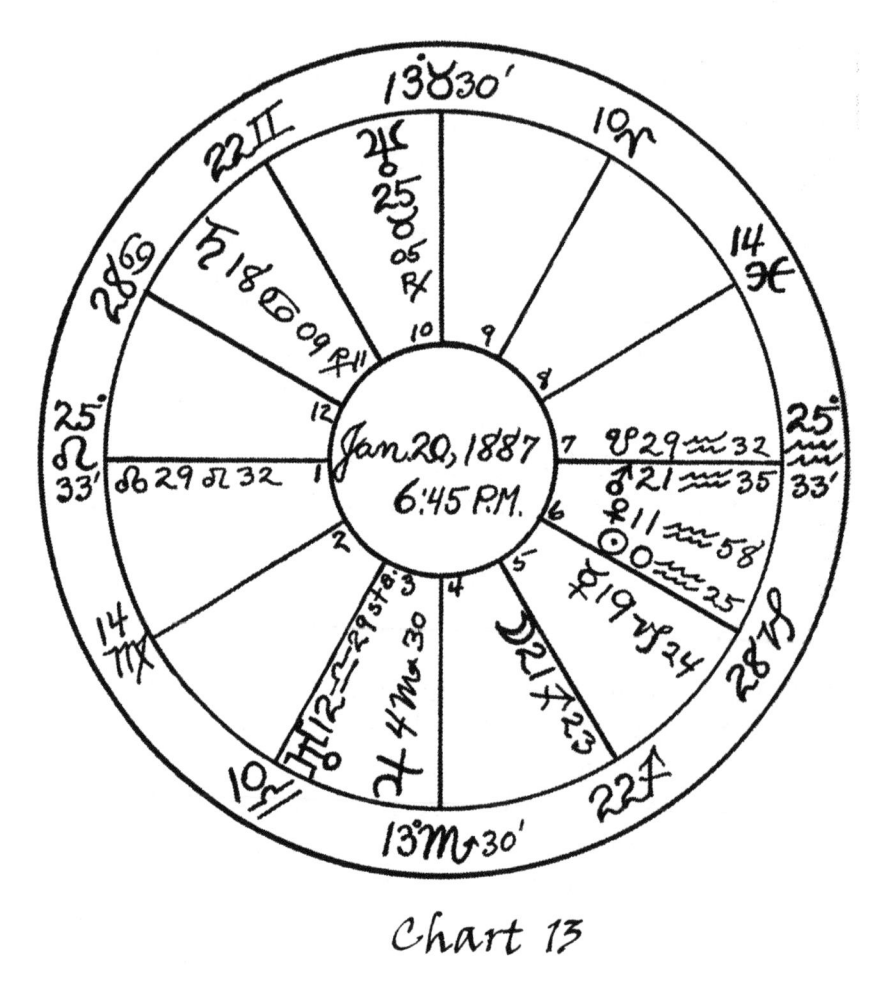

Chart 13

The man who was born May 13th, 1893, when Moon was in Aries, happened to take a wife at whose birth the Sun stood in Leo (see Chart of Horoscope No. 10) and he had hoped, on the basis of astrological laws, for a good intellectual harmony and comradeship. These traits are also extant, and the union externally appears to be very harmonious and peaceful. Personally, however, the wife is very unhappy, because she has been vainly longing for children for many

Character of Lovers

years. Here it would seem, although Jupiter in her horoscope stands at the 5th house cusp, in quartile (90° or square) to Mars and Mercury, as though everything had conspired against her. The husband, for whom the Moon was in opposition to Saturn, of a sudden showed ascetic tendencies; he was a fanatic disciple of Masdasnan for a time, and finally was lost among some sect of so-called bible students,

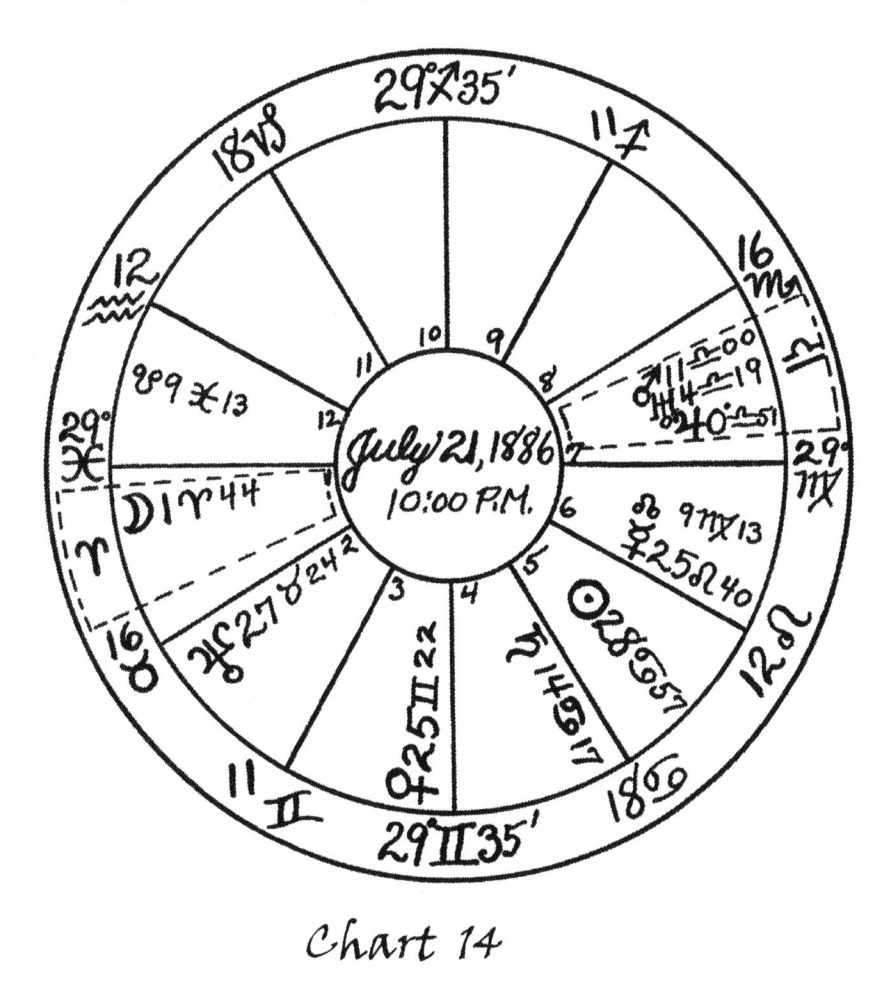

Chart 14

so that the original harmony of the early stages of marriage was transformed into discord.

The Moon in the sign of Taurus bestows something definite, firm and resolute upon the native, enhancing his energies. Since the Moon in Taurus, in the house of Venus, is in the sign of her exaltation, she will accept the influences of this sign, and that which is inconstant, vascillating, and changeable in the Moon-type will transform itself in Taurus in confidence and perseverence. The people in whose horoscope the Moon exerts her influence in Taurus, as in the horoscope of the female born March 22nd, 1874 (Chart No. 4), are industrious to the extreme, and in spite of a very active mind calmly proceeds to practical work. They will make good use of every hour; they will especially be successful when sober and persistent planning is required. They have, of course, a great desire for possessions, wealth, worldly joys and pleasures, they love music and song, or are specially talented for the same. Even in their idealistic and intellectual endeavors they would hardly omit the real and the practical. When people are under the influence of the Moon in Taurus, they are easily won through love and kindliness; they do not, however, tolerate disregard and disparagement, and they easily feel insulted and deeply humiliated. They are really profoundly sincere, they want to be loved, and they can be very tender, affectionate, and attentive. If the Moon receives disharmonious rays, that indicates stubbornness and obstinacy.

People at whose birth the Moon stood in Taurus generally agree best with those in whose horoscope the Sun is in Aries, Taurus, or Virgo.

When the Moon is in quartile to the Sun with a female partner in marriage and when otherwise quartiles of planets prevail in the horoscope of lovers (as in Chart No. 6), insurmountable difficulties will often arise, inasmuch as the types vary in character and they cannot understand each other, or there are cares and worries depressing their lives in common.

The Moon in the sign of Gemini, in the house of Mercury, bestows upon those born under this influence rather an agitated mind, a restless character, continually moving, together with a great desire for change, alterations, news, and travel. Such a craving for diversions and continuous quest for something new will, of course, have its bearing upon love affairs. In such a case, when some choice has been entered into, constant comparisons are made with others, and in consequence there is danger of giddiness, switching between feeling and reason. The Moon in the sign of

Character of Lovers

Gemini will also produce daring of character, willfulness, and artful designs. The mutability and versatile disposition bestowed by the Moon in the sign of Gemini will also make people ready to quickly adapt themselves, in order to take good advantage of all possible chances that seem to promise success. Their affections are very changeable and divided. They need love and tender regard, but intellectual appetizers and time for their hobbies as well. The women that are influenced by the Moon in the sign of Gemini allow reason to dominate alongside of their feelings. In sexual matters they may be devoted, clinging as the vine, endearing and passionate, when they are in the mood to love, but it is also of frequent occurrence with them to be able to keep separate the emotions of body and soul. They are quite excitable in regard to sexual matters, but theirs is less of a wild, animal passion than a capacity to enjoy things in a more refined and intellectual manner, they are magnetically attractive and receptive.

When the Moon is in a double-bodied sign, such as the signs of Sagittarius and Pisces, this will indicate people who during their intercourse will revel as it were in sensual pleasures and indulgences, and still are capable, as their sensual desires are lashed, to give thought to other things than they pursue at the time.

It happens more often, by the way, than one realizes, that loving men and women when in sexual intercourse with those attached to them, will in their minds be with some one else, and that they thus would give vent to tortuous feelings merely to allow their reason or intellect subsequently to better assert itself. In many, perhaps most cases, generally speaking, the appetite for love, and sensual desires are painful rather than enjoyed; but whoever lacks love will become hysteric easily for such time as he has not yet overcome his sexual appetite. Women who must live without love or marriage, whom fate denies a normal life of love or a happy union, or offers no opportunity for sexual contact, are carried by their erotic emotions at times into lofty spheres; they imagine in their ecstatic dreams to see the ideal man, or they commit a kind of "spiritual self-pollution" which, of course, is different than that of the men.

Dr. Otto Weingartner, for instance, has some striking remarks to make about male and female sexuality, in his great work on "Sex and Character," Volume II, as follows:

> "That which has been designated with regard to women as masturbation, originates from a different cause than detumescent desires. The women, and we are here speaking for the first time about a real difference, is far more excitable sexually than the man (I have an answer for this in the third chapter concerning "Fortunes and Love Tragedies" - The Author). Her physiological irritability (not sensibility) is much more pronounced, as far as the sexual sphere is concerned. The fact that the woman is easily irritated sexually may become apparent either in a desire for sexual irritation, or in a peculiar aversion against irritation by contact, such aversion being very irritating, though she may not at all be conscious of it, and for this reason, uneasy and violent. The desire for sexual excitation is in a sense a real sign of easy excitability, inasmuch as it is not one of those wishes which fate, as based in the character of human beings, could never grant. On the contrary, the conditions given indicate such a high degree of ease and willingness, that it would be a matter of course to pass on into a stage of sexual excitability. This stage is desired to be as intensive and perpetuated as possible by the woman; it is otherwise with the man, since the emission brought on by erection causes a natural termination to the desire. That which has been termed onanism of the woman cannot be compared with the actions of the man that have the inherent tendency to interrupt the stage of sexual excitation, the actions of the woman are rather attempts to bring on, to increase, and to prolong such a stage."

At this point I should like to add that women addicted to strong sensual desires often experience far greater enjoyment from the discord of their soul in their dreams and from the revelry of their emotions resulting from imaginations than could be given by a man through body contact for a few flighty moments. Many women indeed, when they no longer feel the encircling arms, imagine they are cast down from all the heavens, and the sorrow over the disillusion is doubly painful.

However, I shall not proceed too far from the subject, *i.e.*, the psychology of love, but return to the influence of the Moon in the various stages.

In Cancer the influence of the Moon is strongest, for that sign is the heaven house of the Moon.

Men as well as women, at whose birth the Moon stood in Cancer, are reputed to show a strong sense of making provision for, and loving, their own home, their home country, of being attached to the mother, of being able to remember everything that was once dear to them, and a strong desire for love and devotion. People that are influenced by the Moon in Cancer are very receptive of, and responsive to, all impressions from without, they readily react upon everything, and well adapt themselves to all given circumstances. Many that are influenced by Moon in Cancer lack confidence in themselves, and a resolute appearance. They are easily overshadowed by others, or they allow themselves to be persuaded towards any action, thus rendering their fortunes subject to many changes, and leading them into new directions. It matters, of course, in which house or heaven area of a horoscope the (sign of the Moon) is located. If the Moon, for instance, stands in the 7th house, which is significant for love and marriage, and of which I shall treat especially, it indicates that sentiments and emotions will change, that there will be sudden separations and illicit contact. Otherwise the Moon is active in good aspects in sextile or triplicity to the Sun, indicating much success in public office. The Moon in the 7th house rather refers to a diversified romance, several marriages, or contacts with female friends other than the legal wife. When the Moon is in the 9th house of a horoscope, as for instance in the Horoscope No. 5, this means a larger mental perspective, by means of much traveling, and a philosophic and religious attitude of life, which is frequently influenced by emotions and sentiments. Persons being influenced by the Moon in this position are subject to many dreams, they are vividly intuitive, sometimes they are adaptable as mediums, and they are able to discover future events. They gather new experiences continually, and they meet with remarkable people while traveling. They often begin a happy romance on their journeys, according to the prevailing aspects. (Chart No. 5.)

People at whose birth the Moon is in Cancer experience their strongest attachment to those at whose birth the Sun is in the sign of Pisces, Taurus, or Scorpio; nevertheless, here, too, the other planet influences should be carefully considered, in order that one might know whether to expect endearing attachments, and whether a friendship is in passing or durable.

In the sign of Leo, the house of the Sun, the influence of the Moon will bestow a strong self-consciousness, some dignity and confidence in one's own resources. At times there is danger of overbearing, of indulgence in luxury and splendor. The emotional life of those influenced by the Moon in Leo is strong, but not to be understood as sentimental. Affinities are usually deep and genuine and when the Moon is in good aspect, friendship and love will be replete with faithfulness and nobility. (For example, see horoscope of June 14th, 1888, Chart No. 11.)

Here the Moon stands in Leo in the 11th house indicating very strong emotions, hopes, and aspirations. The influence is particularly favorable for amicable relations with women.

In the horoscope of the happy husband (Chart No. 7) the Moon is likewise in Leo, but in the 8th house of the horoscope, thus showing rather a proclivity for mysticism and the supersensual, and a form of death which is more or less sudden, because the Moon is in quartile to the Sun and to Mars.

Persons at whose birth the Moon is in Leo as a rule agree best with those at whose birth the Sun stood in Aries or Saggitarius, provided that the harmony is not destroyed by the opposition of influential planets. In scrutinizing and comparing the various horoscopes one will soon discover of what nature the contrasts and conflicting aspects are that are contained in a horoscope.

When the Moon is in the sign of Virgo, in the sign of Mercury, she bestows upon the native a meticulous mind, a propensity for critical distinctions, and intellectual capacity which usually controls one's emotions. These people also have a good sense of reality, they are very deft in all they do, and they chiefly deal with practical interests. Nevertheless they are also interested in literature, art, and science, displaying a knack of grasping details, but losing out of sight the very essence of their study. If the Moon is in the sign of Virgo and well connected with Mercury, in sextile or triplicity, the mental faculties are highly developed. In such a case we find the gift of speaking, a desire for teaching and debating. Even with very good

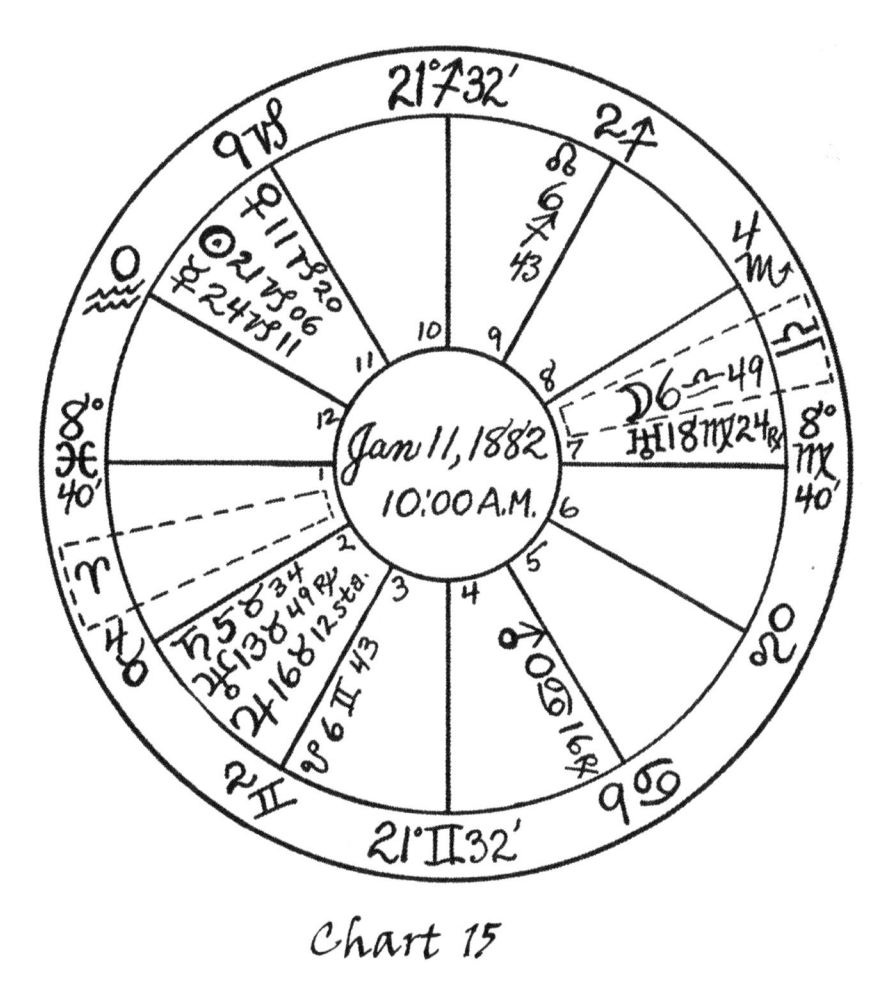

Chart 15

friends they will preferably enter upon vivid discussions, and more tender regards and considerations are crowded into the background. An example of this is furnished in the horoscope of the native born November 3rd, 1904. (Chart No. 18.)

People at whose birth the Moon stood in the sign of Virgo usually mate well according to mind and soul with those at whose birth the Sun was in Aries, Taurus, or in Cancer. If, however, Saturn injects his quartile into influential planets of both signs of the Sun, of lovers, a shadow will be cast even upon the best union, as confirmed by the short married bliss of the young woman born in November.

The Moon in the sign of Libra, in the house of Venus, is noted for the anxiety of men and women always to work for harmonious settlements, to pour oil on the troubled waters, to put the best construction on everything. Those influenced by the Moon in Libra are discreet in their actions, and fair-minded; they like sociability, music, song, they are amiable, gay, engaging in contact with others, and accordingly, have many friends of both sexes. They have a strong propensity for community life.

When the Moon is in the 7th house of a horoscope, as in Chart No. 15, of one born January 11th, 1882, the second wife of a divorcee, whose chart is No. 13, and when the Moon is in opposition to Mars in the 4th house, minor altercations will happen in the "best regulated families." When Mars is retrograde by night, in the 4th house and adversely aspected, it is said to indicate absence of children, a source of remonstrance for the husband.

People at whose birth the Moon is in Libra should unite with such as have the Sun also in sign of Libra in their horoscopes, or in Gemini, or Aquarius. In the horoscope of the husband of this woman, with Moon in Libra, the Sun enters into the sign of Aquarius, so that the two lights of heaven form a triplicity. Venus, moreover, in the horoscope of the husband, stands in Aquarius, in triplicity to the Moon in the wife's horoscope, with the result that this second marriage of the husband, according to his own statement, is peaceful and harmonious, except that he regrets there are no children. This is not surprising, when it is realized that Jupiter, the ruler of his 5th house, of some significance for progeny, forms an opposition from the cusp of the death house of the wife to Saturn and Neptune. I know several men and women of the year 1882 having a like or similar configuration: Saturn, Neptune, Jupiter in Taurus, who remained without child, and whose family life was not happy.

People at whose birth *the Moon stood in the sign of Scorpio*, in the house of Mars, usually appear very attractive to the opposite sex. The influences of the Moon, decreasing in this sign, are less favorable generally for the duration of love and marriage. In the horoscope of a male the adverse aspects to the Moon in Scorpio leads to an unhappy union, in the female horoscope the influences may bring on miscarriages. Sexual excitations and passions of those influenced by the Moon in Scorpio are strong, but not enduring. Energies are dissipated too soon.

When the Moon is well radiated in triplicity to the Sun, efforts are made to bring sensual desires under control of the mind, but if disharmonious aspects towards Venus or towards Mars prevail, these people after all will lack self-control. "The spirit is willing, but the flesh is weak." In matters of love those influenced by Scorpio have their secrets. Generally speaking they also have a propensity for mysticism and occult sciences, but they are also likely to be taciturn and to conceal things, and others will hardly know what to make of them.

When the Moon is in conjunction with Saturn, Mars or Uranus in Scorpio, there is danger of intestinal troubles; women are subject to inflammation of the womb and the ovaries, or there are disturbances of menstruation, whereas men may be subject to infection. The happiness of lovers or married people may thus be dimmed in an unforeseen manner.

People at whose birth the Moon stood in Scorpio, will best agree with those in whose horoscope the Sun stands in the sign of Pisces, Cancer, Virgo, or Capricorn; however, the various aspects should also be considered.

The Moon in the sign of Sagittarius, the house of Jupiter, influences a vivid fantasy, religiosity, frankness and sincerity, unless this influence is disturbed by an aspect of Saturn. Otherwise natives having the Moon in Sagittarius are gay, full of life and confidence, quite vivacious, big-hearted, and noble. They usually show a lively and fiery disposition, they like to travel, engage in sports and outdoor games; they imagine themselves quite independent and at liberty. Moreover their quest for knowledge cannot be satiated, and in a way they are restless of mind. In love affairs those who are influenced by the Moon in Sagittarius are impassionate and quite impulsive, at times too wild and ardent when they act without restraint, and love's emotions amidst encircling arms will vanish away before it has been really tasted.

The preface of love, which for natures having tender feelings is most important and most captivating, will be neglected entirely or passed up by those who are influenced by the Moon in Sagittarius, due to excessive haste and impetuosity, since the emotions of these people flit away too soon. Seldom indeed will both partners become fully satisfied at the same time.

For this reason very many of those that are influenced by the Moon in the sign of Gemini or Sagittarius personally remain dissatisfied, inasmuch as differently constituted natures of two married people, even when in fond embrace, will never agree.

As the sign of Sagittarius and those of Gemini and Pisces are bicorporeal, several marriages are likely, even illicit relations. Witness the Horoscope No. 13 of native born January 20th, 1887. Here the Moon in Sagittarius stands at the cusp of the 5th house, at which point she bestows a strong craving for love and amorous sensitiveness, and also a love for children. An illicit love affair, with consequences, was the cause for the first union, which was very unhappy.

People at whose birth the Moon stood in Sagittarius should unite with such as have the Sun standing in Aries or Leo. Gemini-types should be excepted, since at first great attachment is manifested for them, but that will soon fade away. This fact is proven by the confession I wish to refer to of a woman at whose birth the Sun was in Sagittarius (Chart No. 20), who had been well acquainted with these Gemini-types.

The Moon in Capricorn, in the house of Saturn, standing as she does in the sign of her destruction, will lend her influence rather to deliberate and serious thinking, to steadily following up one's objectives, and to sober action. In a male horoscope the position of the Moon in Capricorn will point to scanty emotions in love affairs. A love pact is rarely made without deliberation; however, the emotions are constant and intense, once there is an attachment.

As a rule men in whose horoscope the Moon is in Capricorn manage to control themselves, and they are capable for a long time to live a chaste and decent life, unless Venus in their horoscope is radiated by Mars or Uranus.

When the moon in Capricorn stands in disharmonious aspects, a person thus influenced will find his path beset with intense difficulties and obstacles, if he would want to realize his plans, which according to his characteristics are quite ambitious.

He will usually have many mishaps in his love affairs; his marriage will be rather temperate, calm and loveless, and entered at a late date.

Women at whose birth the Moon is in Capricorn allow practical and household matters to prevail in their married life, unless other signs indicate a depth of emotion and devotion. They show little desire for romance, and their lack of tender regards and emotional life will often act as a deterrent for their husbands, so that these will look elsewhere for that love which they fail to find with the matter-of-fact wife. At times there are women with profound emotions, but due to the influence of the Moon in Capricorn, they are unable to display them as much as others that are gay and full of life.

People at whose birth the Moon was in Capricorn will best get along with such as have the Sun in Taurus at their birth, or in the sign of Virgo. On the other hand no connections should be attempted with people in whose horoscopes the Sun and several planets stand in Aries, Cancer, or in Libra, as in such cases altercations cannot be avoided.

If the Moon stands too close to the Sun in Capricorn, in quartile to Saturn, or in opposition to Saturn in Cancer, it is reputed to cause celibacy as a rule.

The Moon in Aquarius in the house of Uranus is said to bestow an inclination for occult sciences, mysticism, a predilection for practical psychology, also for highly altruistic endeavors and benevolence in dealing with others. Most of those who are influenced by the Moon in Aquarius are big-hearted in their attitude of life, broadminded, independent, and progressive. They are hardly concerned about what others say about them; they prefer to be guided by their own

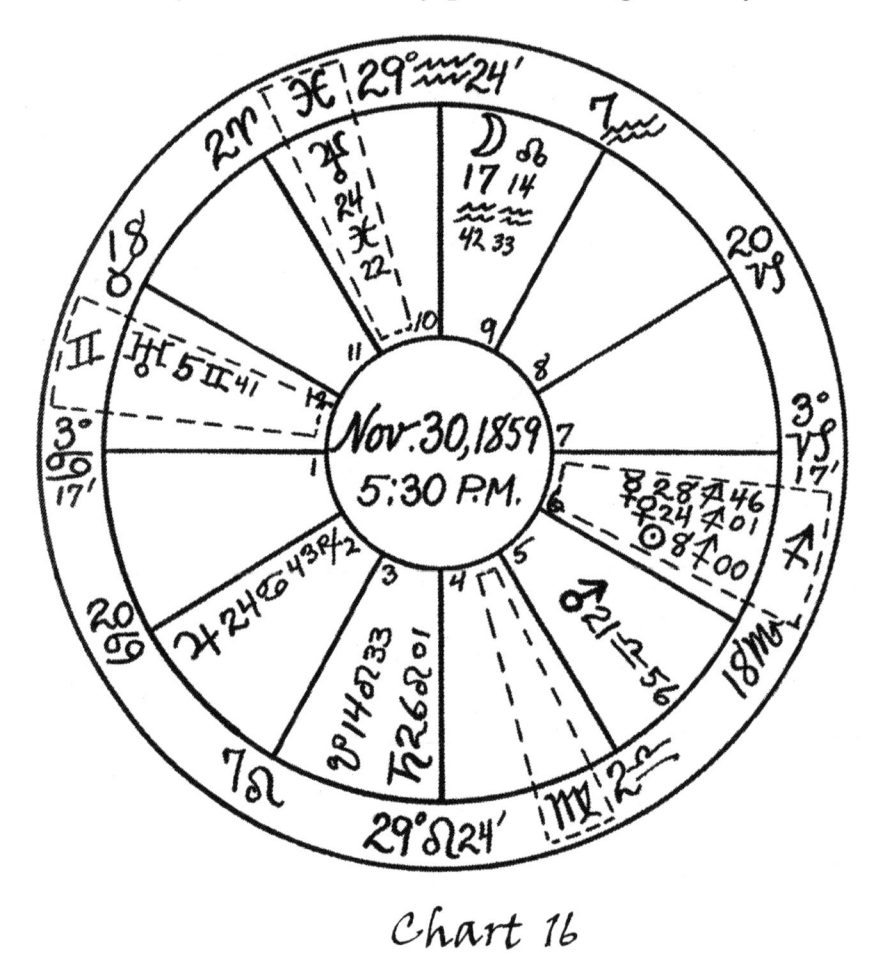

Chart 16

sentiments, and are sometimes eccentric in their Actions, so that it is hard for their neighbors to understand them. If there are any visible obstacles in their love affairs and affections, in the end they do as they please just the same, and they do not mind morals or the law. Their own intuition, their habit of thought and sentiment means more to them than all custom.

Character of Lovers

Chart No. 16 shows the horoscope of a woman born November 30th, 1859, 5:30 P.M., with a tragic history. As Mars in her horoscope in the 5th house stands in triplicity to the Moon in Aquarius, she was plentifully supplied with love. She gave birth to three illegitimate children, but there were unbelievable difficulties presenting themselves against a lawful union with her lover. This may partly be ascribed to the sharp opposition of the Sun to Uranus, which signifies a sudden separation from the lover and a tragic fate. The many planets in bicorporeal signs, Sun, Venus, Mercury in Sagittarius, mysterious Neptune, in the sign of Pisces, and Uranus in the sign of Gemini in the 12th house, perhaps indicate that the native of November has had her full share of love, but otherwise was not especially successful in life. The ruler of the 7th house, Capricorn, is Saturn, who stands in opposition to the Moon, the ruler of the first house. Concerning this there is an astrological rule that the Moon in Aquarius, in hostile aspect to Saturn, in case one of them is ruler of the 7th house, will not permit a marriage. The person referred to managed to make a living with three illegitimate children, and was working in a factory in later years. When, a few years ago, fire destroyed the linen mill at Crimmitschau, where she was employed, she was burned to death with 14 other workers, and her charred remains and of the others were interred together.

The Sun in conjunction with Antares, the many planets in the fire sign Sagittarius, and the Sun in opposition to Uranus, with the Moon in opposition to Saturn, may have determined the forced termination of her work. Jupiter, also, usually proffering happiness and money in the second house, was retrograde, enfeebled in action for good, and being in quartile to Mars in the house of children, could produce but the bare necessities for living. As long as the woman was in her prime, she may have had some income and assistance through charity, but it takes time and money to raise three children, and there was nothing else to do but go to the factory where she found her tragic end. One of her illegitimate children became the second wife of the divorcee (Horoscope No. 13), and furnished us this information. In the horoscope of the daughter of that unhappy woman the tragic fate of the mother is also indicated by Mars in the 4th house (Chart No.

15) in quartile to the Moon. Whoever will take the time to study these horoscopes and to compare them with one another, will find some remarkable complications.

Now we come to the *Moon in the last sign, Pisces,* the heaven house of Neptune and Jupiter. People at whose birth the Moon stood in the sign of Pisces (Charts Nos. 3 and 10), are extremely sensitive and receptive to various influences through which a person may forge ahead, but as well may be dragged down into the abyss. An ardent desire to be active is found with those influenced by the Moon in Pisces only in the event the Sun or Mars occupy a strong position in the horoscope. Otherwise those that are influenced by the Moon in the sign of Pisces are more likely to depend upon others than to be independent. If things go well with them they are rather dreamy and romantic, otherwise they prefer to keep themselves in the background. If, however, the Moon stands in good aspects, they are capable of receiving greater mind energies, and they like to take stock of themselves. Many that are influenced by the Moon in the sign of Pisces are adaptable for mediums, especially when there are planets in a negative sign. In love affairs their sentiments prevail; however, there is a danger of being wholly dependent upon one's own will and thus to lose all self-confidence.

For those at whose birth the Moon stood in the sign of Pisces the most suitable marriage partners are those in whose horoscope the Sun is in the sign of Capricorn, Taurus, Cancer, or Scorpio, and forms a sextile or triplicity to its Moon location or to other influential planets.

After having described the chief influences of the Sun and of the Moon in all twelve signs of the Zodiac, and have referred to a number of examples elucidating the various positions, it might be well to show in the same manner what the Sun and the Moon and all planets indicate in the twelve houses. However, this would grow into a volume three or four times as thick, and might prove too costly for the layman.

The points, as shown, might be sufficient to indicate *the*

Character of Lovers

character of lovers, and I shall thus merely add what effect the planets have in the 7th house of a horoscope, which is quite significant for love and marriage.

It should be simple, after reference has been made to so many charts, to readily see, in sketching a horoscope, whether there is a fortunate or unfortunate planet in the 7th house, and whether to expect happiness in love and marriage, or unhappiness.

Whenever Jupiter, who is supposed to bring luck, *stands in the 7th house* of the horoscope of a man or woman, as in the horoscope charts No. 4 and No. 8, that is a good sign, for this planet's influence shows that the person will not remain alone, and it will bestow happiness for love and marriage. Whether this good fortune is to last a lifetime, may be seen from the position of the progressed planets in the respective years, and by comparing the horoscope of the marriage partner. If Jupiter and Venus oblige with triplicities, as in the horoscope of two happily married people (see Charts No. 7 and No. 8), one may look for the best. If, however, Jupiter receives hostile rays (as in Chart No. 4) from the sun in an opposite sign, or from Mercury, the happiness will not endure, since Jupiter in opposition to the Sun and to Mercury will bring on serious differences of opinion, unpleasant events and court trials which lead to a separation. In spite of Jupiter being in the 7th house the happy marriage of the woman born March 22nd, 1874, Chart No. 4, was followed by a divorce after a few years. This instance shows that one planet alone has no power, nor can it affect permanent happiness, when it is in opposition to the Sun, and when other strong oppositions conspire, such as those of Saturn and Uranus. If in the horoscope of a man there is another planet in hostile aspect in addition to Jupiter, there is in store for him a pretty and charming mate, but marital peace may be disturbed at times.

In addition to the ruler of the 7th house and the planets found in this chapter that are significant for marriage and the communal life, one should also consider how the planets of the horoscope shed rays toward each other, and what position they assume to planet locations in the horoscope of the mate, a great deal of which has already been said in describing aspects. In the horoscope of the woman born July 21st, 1886 (Chart No. 14), Jupiter, for instance, stands in the 7th house, leading to a happy marriage, for the purpose of "giving the child a name." But Jupiter stands in conjunction with Uranus and in opposition to the Moon, so that the union was untenable, and several court trials led to a separation.

When Saturn is in the 7th house of a horoscope, the marriage is contracted rather because of calculations or convenient reasons, at least on the part of one of the mates. There is not much room for cordiality in this case. Even in the event there is fervent love apparent with one of them, or with both, sickness, worries, or ill fortune will be disturbing factors, thus dimming marital happiness.

It is only with people that are highly developed intellectually and morally, that one may assume Saturn in the 7th house of a married person will favor kindred minds and soul affinity, and that the mates have been led together for the fulfillment of higher purposes in life; however, it is quite likely that one of them will quietly grieve because of the other, and that he or she is not fully satisfied.

The planets of the year 1926 had a dangerous significance for many that were born in the years 1874, 1876, 1881 and 1882, with regard to harmony and happiness in married life, inasmuch as Uranus and Saturn or Neptune received hostile rays in their basic horoscope. Uranus in the 7th house of a nativity will effect, according to its respective aspects, sudden attraction or alienation in love affairs and married life. (See horoscope chart No. 14 and No. 18) In these cases Uranus brought a divorce after a brief marriage.

When Uranus is in conjunction with several planets, or with Jupiter in the 7th house of a horoscope, it indicates some romantic love adventures other than the legitimate union, or friendly relations. One will find Jupiter and Uranus at times in the 7th house in the horoscope of artists or in that of persons having a public office, with the result that they were well liked and even adored by many, although this fact need not be a drawback for a happy marriage.

Character of Lovers

When Uranus stands alone in the 7th house of a horoscope, it is quite difficult to find the proper complement for enduring happiness in love and marriage. This influence bestows a measure of freedom and independence; the person cannot bear any limitations or supervision in marriage. Thus, when Sun or Moon, or Sun and Mars, Saturn and Jupiter receive each other's hostile rays in the horoscope of the marriage partners, it is likely there will be a divorce. Uranus will also cause sudden local separations through circumstances between married people or lovers such as they do not expect, and people who are thus influenced will be severely strained in their mind for a time.

Neptune has its own and peculiar action when it stands in the 7th house or at the cusp of this house, which is so important for love and marriage. At first it will cause severe disappointments in youth, heartache, years of unrequited love, and delay of marriage. If Neptune receives hostile rays, it will make contact with shady characters. If, however, Neptune is well aspected (see Chart No. 6), with a triplicity from Uranus, it will lead to love in all variations There will be contacts of a highly intellectual character, valuable relations of a Platonic nature with persons that have made their mark.

Generally speaking, Neptune in the 7th house will rouse affections towards such people that have overcome sensual passions, and have their enjoyment rather cultivating the friendship with cultured and refined people than in amorous sensations. They are also on friendly terms with artists, mystics, intellectual leaders, and persons loving poetry.

When Neptune receives hostile rays it will at times bring on dreadful perturbation of the mind and soul on account of unrequited love or abnormal conditions.

When Mars is in the 7th house, that will indicate a marriage partner who is strong-willed and quarrelsome, so that the peace of the family will often be disturbed in spite of all love and controlled feelings. The violent influence may be softened only through self-possession. Here, too, it much depends upon what aspects or other influences will keep the fire of love or of passions aglow, or mitigate and appease when there are quarrels.

When Mars is well located, the marriage partner will be very bold and active. Mars in the 7th house is shown by the Horoscope No. 12.

Amiable Venus in the 7th house, which is so significant for love and marriage, has a beneficent influence, of course, and fosters peaceful relations and confidence between married people. If however, Venus receives hostile rays of Saturn, there ensues great heartache, and even good will and fervent love will be rewarded with ingratitude. As long as Venus, regardless of good aspects in a basic horoscope, receives a hostile aspect of Saturn or Neptune, the yearning for love will not find as ready a response as is desired, and there will always remain some personal dissatisfaction; until better planet influences will appear.

Mercury in the 7th house is reputed to bestow a smart wife, of a keen mind, and voluble of speech, having more of intellectual faculties than sensuality. Reason will precede sentiment; however, the influences that are contemporary should be considered.

When Mercury in the 7th house is debilitated by Mars or Saturn, it is said that, according to old rules, mysterious events will happen in marriage, so that one will strive to take the other's life, to get rid of him or her, or that he or she will resolve in his mind how to disencumber himself of the unpleasant partner. There is an example of this kind quoted elsewhere, Horoscope No. 17, showing a retrograding and much debilitated Mercury in the 7th House.

When there are no planets in the 7th house of a Horoscope, the Horoscope of the husband should be investigated as to what planet is next to the Moon, and also observe the planets in the vicinity of the Sun in the horoscope of the wife. These planets, being closest to the lights of heaven, are said to also give information as to the traits of the marriage partner. When the Moon in one Horoscope receives the hostile rays of Mars or Saturn, there will be much quarreling in married life; if Jupiter and Venus are hostile to one another, there are differences of opinion about needless expense for luxury and baubles. When Jupiter and Venus are in opposition in the horoscope, the husbands will usually indulge in numerous love affairs or friendships with women; they are very attractive for womankind, and will experience the weal and woe of love in every which way, whether legitimate or not. One example of this is the Horoscope of Wolfang Goethe, see the Chart in my book, entitled, "The Golden Bridge to the World of Stars," page 104, and his complete biography in the greater volume, entitled, "Historic and Contemporary Character Sketches According to Manuscripts, Picture, Nativity, and Life Work of Prominent Thinkers and Poets." In a Horoscope contained in this book, of February 26, 1861, No. 6, we find an exact opposition of Jupiter, 20 degrees Leo at the cusp of the 7th house, to Venus in 18 degrees Aquarius, which indicates a versatile love affair with a tinge of the romantic.

In this instance Saturn and the Moon in the 7th house also point to the early loss of the wife, and several marriages. Two marriages are already recorded in the history of this man; a third is desired but has not been consummated because of illness and lack of response.

The fortunes of this person have become quite tragic through quartiles acting restrictively.

The attentive readers will, accordingly, have realized that happiness in love and marriage, or harmonious and friendly relations are to be expected, when there are beneficent planets in the 7th house of a Horoscope, or when the rulers of this house of love and marriage are found in good aspects in one's own horoscope and to planets in the Horoscope of those that are very dear to them. The rulers of the various signs can be ascertained from the description on Page 18, *e.g.*, the ruler of the sign of Aries is Mars, of Taurus, Venus, of the sign of Gemini, Mercury, etc.

To repeat: It is especially fortunate when in the Horoscope of lovers the Sun or Moon stand at the identical place in the Zodiac, or at an exact distance of 120 degrees, or, when the heaven lights Sun and Moon form a harmonious aspect to Mars, to Venus, Jupiter, or Uranus. In such cases there are happy prospects for marriage.

Very seldom, however, a Horoscope will be found which is completely free from repulsive aspects; and there are but few marriages which are permanently and completely happy and free from worries, even though certain planets will point to happy love and marriage, such as the triplicities of Jupiter and Venus in the two Horoscopes, Nos. 7 and 8. In the event Sun and Moon well radiate each other in the basic Horoscopes of lovers, hostile counter-currents will, nevertheless, occur from progressions in the course of the years, towards planet locations of the marriage partners, and it may come to pass that people who had been really happy in the first few years of marriage will suddenly realize they are not understood, or are drifting apart, as their minds develop at variance. The original love becomes extinct. This will especially happen often during good aspects of the Sun and Venus. That love was based upon sensuality and superficial affections, and personally they suddenly become alienated. Those, who subsequently realize it all, will tell themselves, "How could I ever be so foolish as to love this woman / or this man?"

This realization, of course, always comes too late, and Astrology will thus explain matters, but bring little relief; nevertheless it is worth the trial to get at the bottom of things, to protect one's self of disappointments.

To complete this analysis, I shall here refer to an excerpt taken from an old volume, showing how any person might prognosticate his impending good or ill fortune. The book is published by Gottlieb Nicolai, 1737, especially treating planets in the 7th house, which I do not want to withhold from my male and female readers, inasmuch as many of these rules, as any one may check them up, to this day appear to be adequate. I shall quote the rules verbatim, changing only the spelling, and adding a few remarks of my own observation.

"Saturn in the 7th house, if in his exaltation, or in his own sign, promises rich women, but also bitter enemies, much trouble in marriage, angry words with bad women or others, moreover, Saturn will cause hard diseases, such as podagra, red diarrhea, hemorrhoids, and other disagreeable conditions."

Applying this rule, we should watch the aspects of Saturn. Usually Saturn will furnish much trouble and labor, even when marriage is contracted for considerations of reason or money, and it will be difficult to arrive at a pleasant, happy, or carefree union (Chart No. 6). If the Moon's South Node still pairs with Saturn in the 7th house, grave diseases are likely, or the death of the wife. Witness, the Horoscope of a gentleman, personally known to me, who was married but a few months, and for whom it is exceedingly difficult to arrive at harmony and happiness in love and marriage.

> "Jupiter in the 7th house promises two or three beautiful, pious, and rich wives, a victory over enemies, honor and happiness in old age."

This rule, also taken from the gray ages, must likewise be taken with a grain of salt. I know a considerable number of gentlemen and ladies of our day, at whose birth Jupiter stood in the 7th house, but I observed the two qualifications seldom united with regard to the wife. Either the bride was very pretty, or rich, rarely both together. Many wives of husbands, at whose birth Jupiter stood in the 7th house, did indeed receive a good dower, or were fitted out well. However, we rather mean something else today with riches than they did formerly. The old rule seems to hold good only when Jupiter is alone in the 7th house, well aspected, (as in Chart No. 8); if, however, Jupiter is in opposition to the Sun (Chart No. 4), this significance is negated, as I explained in the previous chapter.

When Jupiter shares a place with Uranus in the 7th house, one may expect a happy romance, in general, marriage; but this may be quickly destroyed, as the examples taken from life tell us. Uranus, not known by the ancients, has many and great surprises in store in our times, alternating weal and woe, but eventually it will be realized that these changes were necessary for future development.

> "Mars in the 7th house threatens with evil, recalcitrant, or sick husbands, or heavy expenses on account of love and marriage. Mars signifies labor and trouble, enmities, law suits, and precarious situations."

The verdict concerning the influence of Mars should not be taken too seriously. It may happen that Mars, as a ruler of the 7th house, will carry much quarreling and discord into marriage, but it may be possible for either partner to mitigate the influence of Mars by self-possession and patience.

"The Sun in the 7th house means a fashionable wedding, or marrying into high society, honor in old age, but also hostility or opposition from the government or influential men."

Applying this rule it may depend upon the influence dominating the entire Horoscope. At any rate it seems to bold good in many cases that men and women in whose Horoscope the Sun is in the 7th house may require as a partner some well esteemed person, and they may establish a pleasant home. At times the influence of the Sun will force a wider sphere of public activity.

When the Sun is in the 7th house of a Horoscope, the word of Schiller does not apply at all:

"The chaste housewife at home is supreme."

They are seldom satisfied in the precincts of a home, or in poverty; they prefer to let their light shine, to do big things, or come before the public.

If the husband is not able to so shape environments that they might lead a sinecure life, as befitting their individuality, and have many pursuits, they will rather stand on their own feet and take up the struggle for existence in order to make *progress*.

They thus give expression to a virile character; they yearn for freedom and independence. With many women engaged in a calling, or otherwise employed, and relying upon their own resources, the Sun is found in the 7th house of their nativity.

Personally I also belong to the women in whose Horoscope the Sun radiates the 7th house, and heaven thus far has neither bestowed a husband prominent in society nor one of nobility -- a number of very good friends, to be sure, but also quite a few there are jealous, and some enemies. Generally speaking I get along far better without a husband.

From all the confessions of lovers, of sufferers, or bachelors, as contained in this volume, one may see that the ancient statements, that have come to us from past centuries, concerning the locations of planets in the various heaven houses need a thorough revision, or check-up, that not every rule can be taken as it stands, but that in every case it may furnish but a few indicative points.

It will be more to the point to say that the position of the Sun in the 7th house much rather promises success in public office than in the restricted family circle, and that, whenever some one whose individuality is quite pronounced finds himself hemmed in, people give more thought to sacrificing their own home than to tolerate the will of another.

"Venus in the 7th house promises benign, pretty, and wealthy women."

I have often found this rule confirmed; however, since wealth and beauty are perishable, the position of Venus in the 7th house of a male Horoscope is not in itself a voucher for a permanently successful union, particularly when Venus receives hostile rays of Uranus and Mars. If Venus receives good aspects of Mars and Jupiter, in the 7th house, the respective person, male or female, will be the object of much love and adoration

If Venus, on the other hand, is in quartile with Neptune (as in Chart No. 19), happiness in love is doubtful. The person referred to before rather recently complained again that he is not fortunate in love affairs, and he regrets that he was not married for at least half a year. He writes that the best time of his life had been during the war, when he had been buried in the debris and had been seriously ill in the hospital. During this period some nurse had at least stroked his hair at times, whereas his life had otherwise been miserable and devoid of love.

The Moon's South Node in the 7th house, and Jupiter in quartile to Mars, to Saturn and to the Sun, will in this instance deny and retard marriage, all this in spite of the presence of Venus in the 7th house. The numerous planets in the 8th house of this horoscope likewise do not favor a successful romance on this earth, and rather cause one to yearn for the great beyond, or to brood over committing suicide. Nevertheless, these are only sentiments; as soon as some light is shining brightly there is another lease on life.

> "Mercury in the 7th house indicates mathematical wizards, clerks, and industrious people, but these are usually willful, and sometimes sickly. In the sign of Saturn or Mars (Capricorn, Aries, or Scorpio) Mercury will produce maids, tavern keepers, and couplers, people that would do some profiteering in love or marriage affairs. When Mars or Saturn is also present, the native had better beware of his enemies, lest he be murdered by them, and he had better have a care lest he himself becomes the murderer of the husband or wife."

This rule needs verification, and it would be necessary to collect a considerable mass of dates of birth of those who sought to take the life of the marriage partner, or threatened to do so, or have murdered the partner, or were murdered by the mate. As a consequence many people, perhaps, will be careful in the future not to become too intimate with such as have a criminal turn of mind. Among many hundreds of Horoscopes in my collection I found but few in which Mercury in the 7th house was thus critically radiated, and had a tragic effect. One example I cannot refrain from producing at this point, inasmuch as it did largely confirm the above rule. In this Horoscope (Chart No. 17), Mercury, being retrograde in the 7th house, forms a quartile to Mars and Uranus (from an angle of about 90 degrees), and there are other planetary positions in this horoscope which make for mysterious happenings, such as Neptune in conjunction with the Moon, and both in formative opposition to Jupiter, who is retrograde in the 11th house.

The woman born in this critical combination of planets was unhappily married, incurred the danger of being poisoned by a rival, and experienced all the torments of an unrequited love.

I shall permit this woman to tell her own story, beginning from her youth:

Character of Lovers

"I was said to have been born July 5th, 1888, 6 P.M., in 0. Ammerseegegend, about 22 kilometers from Munich, of an unmarried mother. At the age of three months I was taken to the parents of my mother, who reared me, while my mother did not contribute a cent. The grandparents were poor people; the grandfather was a day laborer with wages at 3 marks per day. The

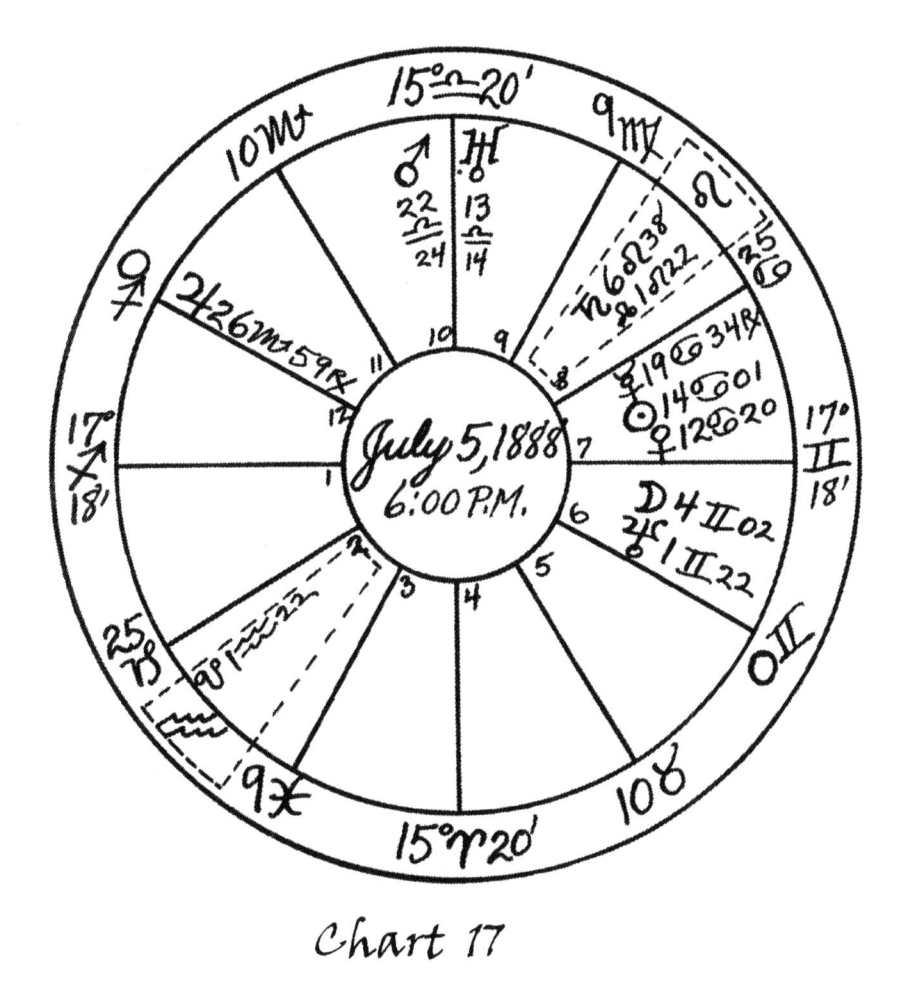

Chart 17

grandmother was sewing, yet my childhood received its protection through my good grandmother, who had a sunny disposition and had a fairly good education, despite her poverty.

At seven or eight years I contracted a severe case of pneumonia. I went to a village school until I was thirteen, was very gifted, only that

I was not interested in catechism nor in grammar. When I finished school I was put to work with a baker at the same place, and stayed there for five years. In the meantime there was an increase of five children, and plenty to do in consequence. As the pay of 10 marks per month was not enough I changed my work. I was with a business firm for two years. Then I went to Munich to a butcher shop, but was there but four months on account of being unable to get along. My next position was with an instructor at a high school.

After four months I received news of my grandmother that she had a fracture of her foot. I resigned my position at once, to take care of my good grandmother. The grandfather had died in the meantime.

In 1909 I became acquainted with my husband, Ernest (born October 11th, 1886, the hour is unknown), who had come into our house to visit my grandmother. We began a love affair, and this was not without consequences. Marriage was delayed until late in fall, due to untoward conditions. Our wedding took place on a Saturday, November 20th, 1909. Exactly eight days later, November 28,190, we had a peculiar visitor, a state's attorney and investigator, who arrested the husband I had just married. Court proceedings for fraud ended with a penalty of incarceration for a year and eight days. On the day my husband was unexpectedly taken away I fell down the stairs with a bucket of water. Apparently there was no damage with the exception of a big boil on my head, unless the expected child received damage.

My little daughter arrived December 9th, 1909, 10:30 P.M., at the women's hospital at Munich, where I had taken refuge

During the time my husband was serving his term in prison I stayed with my grandmother in daytime, and we sewed together. We had secured a modest household, but had lost everything, as everything had been confiscated that my husband had. This evil year passed along eventually; every day ended with a 'Praise to the Lord, another day less.'

My husband returned during the Christmas week of 1910, broken in spirit. I encouraged him; everything would and must be all right. In February, 1911, and again in July of the same year, we moved, again in November to Dresden. There my husband tried to start a business, which in 1912 was established by and by. In the beginning of March, 1913, our little daughter was operated upon because of hip trouble; the hip was dislocated by a fall from the stairway, perhaps my own mishap might have been at the bottom of this when I was with child. It took a good half year before the plaster cast could be removed from the little martyr; even then the child could not walk because of its weakness.

In January, 1914, my husband was expelled from Dresden. He had trouble with the courts, of course, and that was superimposed by a bad report and a previous jail sentence. From Dresden we went to live in Bavaria, where I started a business myself in cosmetics. My business prospered beyond all expectations; even when war broke out in August it did not injure the business much to speak of. However, on March 6th, 1915, my business was subjected to an investigation, as ordered by the state's attorney. After having much ado back and forth everything was released again, and the investigation was stopped.

On May 25th, 1915, my husband had intimate relations with a waitress, and the consequences were apparent. He was hailed into court accordingly in 1916, to attend to his paternal duties. What else could I do, when the distracted sinner pleaded, 'Kate, help me, please, do not desert me.' I came to his aid. I went to court myself and arranged with the mother of the child for a cash settlement, which I paid in July of the current year.

I saw the child, it was a frail girl, the poor thing was an object of pity. During the years of war there were no other disturbances, my husband was not drafted because of debility. In 1919 my husband visited with a local family, became intimate with the woman, and the secret love affair began. The husband of that woman was arrested for embezzlement, in which his wife was chiefly involved. For nine months, she too was held for investigation. My worst sorrows now began for me in 1921.

This woman had a premature birth on August 2nd. By September 19th it gradually dawned on me what was going on, although I rather refused to believe it. However, this woman, born March 24th, 1886, herself opened my eyes. For the entire summer I was quite depressed, joyless, a physical wreck through disorders of the stomach. I always said to my husband, 'I am anxious to know what is coming now. I don't know what is the matter with me.' I was unhappy unto death, and like an owl I stayed in my room. The husband of this woman next came to me with disclosures, with facts I should have seen long ago. From this moment, as these disclosures were made, my husband made no pretense any more. He as well as that woman were seen in public together, neither cared whether or not there were still marital ties. In the meantime, already in the course of the summer, I was completely enfeebled and became paralyzed at the extremities from eating fruitcake which the adulteress had mixed with atropine. No one could explain at first what the cause of it was, until one day her own husband had difficulties in swallowing his food and found some kernels in the cup of coffee which his wife had served. He took these kernels to the physician, who ascertained them to contain atropine. Whereupon the woman was jailed again for attempt at poisoning.

After administering an antidote my stomach gradually improved, but my nerves had wholly collapsed, and daily I entertained thoughts of suicide. It was my child that detained me from it.

From September, 1921, to Easter, of 1922, I was but a shade, and my hair turned all gray. From April 1 I again attended to my business myself.

In 1922 the woman was divorced from her husband, who committed the children to her. It was my husband who cared for them, and in the meanwhile he was with her all the time in the third floor of the same building, and I was alone in the store

Until August 1st, 1922, I tolerated this thing going on in the same building, but now my patience was exhausted. I went to the chief of police and asked that this woman be evicted and banned from the city. Three days later an officer called for her at the house and sent her over the border.

I was rid of her, as far as the house and business was

concerned, but otherwise she clung all the more tenaciously to my husband. He was with her every day until midnight.

In 1923 the two went together to annual fairs and expositions. They tour the country together to this day. Recently in spring I obtained a divorce from my husband. Why should I continue to pose as his wife, now that he shows no concern any more for his child, much less for me. Towards last he even committed brutalities, to which he had been instigated by that woman.

Now to say a word about myself. In spite of it all, I loved my husband dearly. I could have forgiven, though not forgotten everything. Formerly he was kind and good, even industrious, and, despite his profligacy, he was concerned about his family. Even though we were of different dispositions, things might not have come to such a pass had not this woman led him on and captured him for herself by her perversities.

Since he offered so little resistance to good and bad influences, he abandoned himself. Perhaps today he is unhappier than I am.

I now consider the affair settled; today I can enjoy life again, and I am not angry at my husband, for I cannot hate him. Outside in nature I find my creator, the Lord of heaven and earth, in every flower, embodied in every living being; all this is a revelation to me. ..."

She added a few religious observations.

I have quoted the report of this woman word for word, because the communications are clearly reflected in the horoscope referred to. Here we have a fate that is especially tragic, and the old rule concerning the position of Mercury in the 7th house in quartile to Mars is plainly confirmed. It is remarkable that even Jupiter, in control of birth, or as a ruler of the rising sign of Sagittarius, should form an opposition to the Moon and to mysterious Neptune. It is also not surprising that the Sun and Venus form a quartile to Uranus, thus verifying astrologically the scandals, jealousies and convulsions of this union up to the separation from the husband. All this will be still more plausible when the planetary configurations on the birthdays of the pair that was criminally constituted are searched for the most important planet positions and compared with those of the deceived woman.

In the horoscope of the deceiver and adulterer, who had been arrested very soon after the wedding, and who was born October 11th, 1886, we find Venus, Uranus and Jupiter in conjunction between the 4th and the 16th degrees in Libra -- *i.e.*, where Uranus stands in the horoscope of the deceived woman (Chart No. 17), and this planet group is in quartile to Venus, Sun, and Mercury in the 7th house of the wife.

Moreover, in the horoscope of the perfidious husband there is also Saturn 22 degrees in Cancer, accordingly, in quartile to Mars and Mercury, and Neptune is 27 degrees Taurus in opposition to Jupiter in the horoscope of the wife. It is thus quite plausible astrologically why this woman was obliged to suffer as much from the beginning, and that her life was endangered from poisoning.

In the horoscope of the adulteress that had been found guilty of poisoning, we find Jupiter and Uranus between 1st and 5th degree Libra in opposition to the Sun in Aries and in an exact quartile to Saturn in the first degree Cancer. These aspects of Jupiter and Saturn in quartile to the Sun, restrictive in their action, verify the repeated confinement in jail, whereas Jupiter and Uranus in opposition to the Sun are corroborative aspects for affecting a divorce and for the many removals.

Anyone who would convince himself of the position of these planets, will find the planet positions well indicated in the ephemeredes of 1886.

As to the position of the Moon in the 7th house of a Horoscope, the astrological rules of ancient and modern treatises agree with what has been said in the present chapter. The Moon in the 7th house is also said to indicate that the native will not always stay in his country, and that he will be subjected to many dangers and quarrels. (See Chart No. 6.)

In evil aspects to Saturn and Mars the Moon prevents

marriage or will bring about a great calamity and mishaps in married life. If, however, the Moon is radiated by Jupiter or by Venus, or has otherwise a good position, this indicates several wives and overcoming the enemies.

The "Moon's North Node," or "Dragon's Head," in the 7th house (as in Chart No. 7) has been designated as favorable from ancient times, promising happiness in marriage and quiet old age; the Moon's South Node, or "Dragon's Tail," on the contrary (as in Charts No. 3, 13, and 19), is said to threaten with public enemies, disgust of marred life, and early loss of the wives through divorce or death.

Both men, in fact (No. 3 and 13), in whose Horoscope there is the Moon's South Node in the 7th house, have been separated from their first wives, and married again, whereas the latter (No. 19) still yearns for love in vain.

It often happens that, when several planets are present in the 7th house of a Horoscope, at least one of the marriages will be happy or tolerable, after sad experiences.

I trust that this description and compilation of all influences of Sun and Moon in the various signs of the Zodiac, the explanation of the meaning of all planets in the 7th house of a Horoscope, as well as consideration of discordant aspects on the basis of the various planetary positions, will be very instructive and useful for most readers, and that everyone who already has a Horoscope chart will get an idea how to interpret a Horoscope, and what should be considered and estimated. It is understood that in citing examples I could give special mention only to the points that are significant for love and marriage. However, the third chapter, entitled "Fortunes and Love Tragedies," will portray a few interesting character sketches and narratives of distressing events.

It will be clear to many that the love affairs of numerous people are changeable and tragic, and that their own fortunes are not the worst at all.

No doubt there is love of a rare kind in our days which suffers everything and still bears, of which Wolfgang Goethe speaks:

*"That is true love which always remains true to itself,
Whether it is granted everything, or everything denied."*

I should almost want to make the assertion that such a love which always remains the same is seldom found with anybody, but much less in a union which has been contracted by persons of a different caliber, since everything is subject to changes, sentiments and moods through the influence of superior powers and astral currents. Nevertheless, people will time and again believe in friendship, happiness, and peace of heart, since:

*"Love remains the golden ladder
On which the heart mounts into heaven."*

Character of Lovers

Fortunes and Love Tragedies

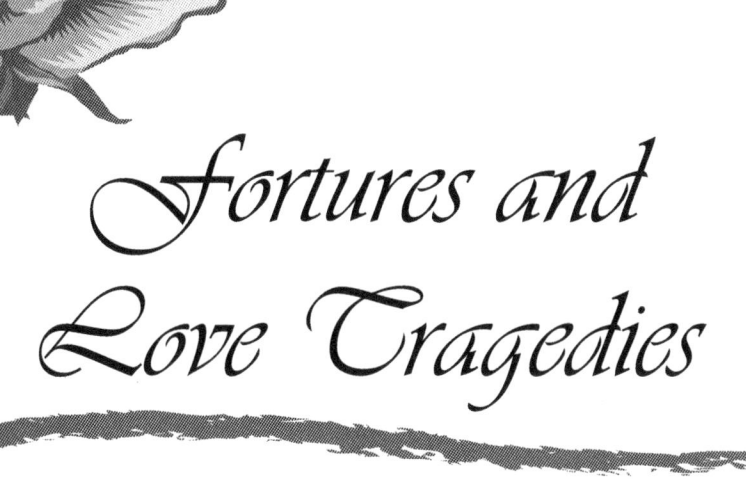

"When Love awakens, tragedy will lift up its sublime face. The love struggle of the powers of the universe, and their contradiction, the paths of good and evil planets pierce the human heart."

—Jos. August Lux.

Before I enter upon the fortunes and love tragedies of individuals, and explain the planetary positions of the Horoscope in their bearing upon good or evil fortunes, I should like to say a few words about love affairs and married life of our days.

In perusing modern literature and taking a cross-cut of life, it is apparent that today opinions differ entirely from those of several decades ago, or even centuries ago, and that many changes have taken place. Womankind also has become emancipated, and, sad to say, indeed, with the exception of the fashionable women, their persistent economic struggles and worries do not permit them as much time as formerly, to give vent to their truly feminine emotions. The exigencies of the times oblige all, men as well as women, to do less of dreaming and more of work, regardless of all the yearning for love, which is perhaps dominant in the human breast, to take up the battle for existence, and to bravely overcome all discords and conflicts.

A few years ago it was the talk of the day as to who was

more passionate and anxious for love, the man or the woman, and opinions differed widely. I should like to say a word on this topic, which always is a live one.

It cannot be maintained that the desire for contact with the other sex is more prominent with the men than with the women, or vice versa, that the emotional life, or sensuality, of the women is greater than that of men. Ardent emotions and desires are entirely individual, since every human being has something in him of the masculine and the feminine, and since there are just as many active women, with a strong, masculine disposition, as there are weakly or "effeminate" men.

In our days of emancipation, and the shortage of men, as produced by the world war, many women who in normal times and in better circumstances would have been compliant characters have been compelled, through life's battles, to become brave and independent, in order not to succumb in the struggle for existence. Stories have been related to me telling of women who on the spur of the moment developed into real heroines or martyrs, at times when men would lose courage. It has been ascertained by statistics that thousands have committed suicide in the last few years, when they thought they could no longer bear a life of worries or the battle for eking out a mere existence.

Numerous husbands who were facing ruin during and after the inflation were on the verge of despair, and they would have perished if they would not have had energetic and encouraging wives, who always knew a way out.

As a rule the women can more easily adapt themselves -- even when they have seen better days -- to changed and pitiful conditions than men can.

I know of the wives of captains who formerly were being spoiled and coddled, but who resolutely faced the music of bitter want, dismissed their servants, applied the broom and scrubbing brush, and did not shun any work of any kind, whereas on the other hand their men, who courageously faced death in the trenches, suddenly faltered, not knowing what to do.

Formerly the wives depended exclusively upon the husbands, who provided for them; today that is not the case. Many thousands of women today are obliged to work for a living. The marital unions are few in which the wife attends to her household duties only, and may rely upon the masculine protector.

Formerly the women bowed to the will of their husbands, whether they were happy or unhappy in so doing, and in mute grief may have had thoughts such as these:

> *"I am a woman, I must quietly bear everything,*
> *I must not battle for my love, nor dare,*
> *I must not send a ray from my heart,*
> *To tell him what has long been glowing and trembling there, ...*
> *I am a woman. What has remained unto me?*
> *Nothing, except to quietly love, but always to love him."*

The day has long passed for that quiet and lasting love. Everything is subject to change in our days, and the duration of love and of marriage pacts is not an exception. Our generation is fleeting, racing, rapidly changing; he who would give vent to his sentiments and emotions might possibly be declared old-fashioned.

There may be a few exceptions here and there, people who are truly and affectionately attached to one another to the end of their days, but they are very rare.

Since the dreadful period of the world war, and the economic collapse of our days, the conceptions about love and marriage have changed a great deal; even lovers having the best of intentions to establish a well ordered household, a delightful home, are prevented from doing so through shortage of dwellings, and the perversity of fortune. Before they succeeded in making themselves a cozy home, they often would separate, or they lost patience.

In these our cheerless days there was nothing left for the women and the girls to do but to compete with the man. It is sad enough that matters came to such a pass. This will necessarily continue for a number of years, until in the course of things an equitable solution is found, and life has been made easier for those who still have a hard struggle.

There have also been a number of women who formerly had nothing of the masculine about themselves, who considered themselves very happy to be entirely feminine and to hear nothing about life's struggles, but the exigencies of the times compelled them, if they would not perish, to transmute original meekness and devotion into making provision for, and sharing things in common with, their dearly loved husbands.

Present circumstances are so devoid of cheer that people truly loving each other, anxious to marry, perhaps destined for one another by nature, cannot contract a union because of the dearth of flats and the economic crisis still obtaining, whereas other people that have become alienated from one another, are obliged to live together, although their affections belong to others, just because the respective parties cannot find a place to rent.

It even happens in our days that such as had been unhappily married and had obtained a divorce would come to an agreement that both parties would take up into their home their respective sweethearts, and all would form a company by threes or fours.

These quadrangle arrangements, according to which divorced parties who were not able at once to find quarters would agree to place their respective sweethearts into a common home, are reputed to be even congenial; at any rate they are less painful than these well-known "triangles," in which only one of the parties found a sweetheart.

When there are two and two together they will not harp at each other, nor would they have the right to be jealous of one another. Besides, each pair hopes some time to find suitable quarters, even though they now would have to make the best of it.

All these quaint conditions are the results of the economical stress of our days. One should, therefore, try to understand these anomalous combinations and exercise fair judgment.

With reference to these peculiar, though not rare cohabitations of lovers within contact of the divorcees, and in consideration of the remarkably friendly relations in free love, one should not forget that even in this respect there is a significance in special planetary configurations.

The very ancient rules of past centuries, of which I reproduced a number for verification, should not any longer be applied without proper consideration. The statements concerning planet locations in the various heaven houses, generally speaking, are correct; for instance, that Jupiter in the 7th house causes a happy marriage (see Chart of Horoscope of June 12th, 1897, Chart No. 8), but please note how the other planets stand, in order to tell whether the happiness will endure.

Even when two marriage partners agree wonderfully, and are thus happy in their love, it is still possible to mar such happiness with some depression or sorrow. I merely want to say that a Horoscope should never be judged one-sidedly, that is, according to only one planet which is well radiated, if you would find out the truth. There are striking triplicities which are only a blind, if the counter-currents are overlooked. There are no Horoscopes at all containing only good aspects; sooner or later there will be a serious trial period for everyone. For this reason I have purposely selected Horoscopes from the wealth of my material as would contain very conflicting aspects, in order to point out for the beginner the difficulties in interpreting a Horoscope.

It is quite easy for a layman or for one taking but a superficial view to say, "Oh, well, this statement does not hold good with me," or, "This planet has not the usual effect"; it is not so easy to investigate why it is otherwise with a good many things, as there is no rule without an exception.

It was not an easy matter at all to furnish for this volume at least a few Horoscopes of people that say of themselves that they are truly happy. Everywhere abounded the "ifs" and "buts," and, "if this or that would not be, we could be happy." Apparently the statement of Bo Yin Ra, the author of an instructive book, entitled "Marriage," is correct when he says, "There never yet was a union which was far removed from all sorrow and knew of joys only."

Despite all circumspection and questioning on my part among my many acquaintances, and notwithstanding my search among the charts of my archives, I have found only the Horoscopes No. 7 and No. 8, of two who were happily married and according to their own statements wonderfully agreed with one another.

There is a marvelous quotation from Grillparzer, from his Sapho I, which will fit in this case:

*"Such is the marvelous power of love
That it ennobles that which is touched by her breath,
Similar to the sun, whose golden ray
Will even change into gold the clouds of a storm."*

In all other marriages there always seems to be something left to be desired. The marriage partners having the Horoscopes No. 9 and No. 10, in which Sun and Moon have good alternating action, could be happier, were the union, as is being anxiously desired by the wife, blessed with children. However, in this case all means failed, even following the method of Frank Glahn for astrological counsel, *i.e.* the assumption that pregnancy is best possible when the Moon passes over the ascendant or descendant, *i.e.* over the 1st or 7th cusp of the Horoscope. Perhaps the rule fails in this case because in the Horoscope of the husband (Chart No. 9) the Moon, which is quite significant for pregnancy, is in opposition to Saturn, which fact would rather indicate according to old astrological rules lonesomeness and celibacy. Perhaps the woman would have children, had she married some one else. Well, the end of all days has not yet come, and she may yet have her wish.

We shall now examine the Horoscopes No. 11 and No. 12 of two people who had several children, and who found the Glahn method correct. Neither of them did anything to prevent pregnancy, but let nature have her way. The union of these two, of whom the husband was born June 14th, 1888, the wife December 27th, 1890, cannot be called particularly happy; however, here are two people that knew something about Astrological laws from their early youth, and they endeavor to overcome their disharmonious moods as much as possible.

In comparing both Horoscopes Nos. 11 and 12 we find there is an absence of really hostile influences towards one another, but on the other hand there is no indication of very favorable combinations, except the triplicities of Mars, Uranus in the sign of Libra in triplicity to Jupiter in the Horoscope of the wife.

These aspects are certainly quite significant for a legitimate union deliberately entered upon.

I put a question to the husband, whom I knew from his youth, how he fared in his married life despite a few contradictory aspects and the position of Mars in the 7th house of the Horoscope of his wife, and he states a few things that may be quite instructive for many readers:

"Perhaps it is most important that the ascendant of my wife at the position of the Moon of my horoscope is in Leo, and it was this configuration which brought us together.

The Moon in particular, of my Horoscope, is very important for relations with the feminine. The Moon is in Leo in the 11th house, and in numerous cases I can ascertain that my friends and acquaintances are subject to a strong influence of Leo.

With my wife the marital union is shown in the ascendant sign of Leo. My mother as well as several lady friends have the Sun in the 2nd or 3rd decanate Leo. (This means the second and last third of the sign.) Which influences led to our union? Strictly speaking it was a mutual affection. Both of us were quite young when we became acquainted, but we were old enough to realize there were mutual affections. It was a case of love at first sight.

Since neither of us is inclined to be flighty we remained true to one another, and we were married. In spite of the Leo influence in the ascendant my wife has a sober and matter-of-fact disposition, due to the Sun in Capricorn (see characteristics of Capricorn, page 55 -- the author), and the position of the planets rather to the westward.

She lacks a great deal in ability to adapt herself; she easily feels herself slighted, or insulted, and in such cases she is disgruntled and out of sorts. This may be the fault of the prevalence of negative signs, as well as of the fact that the faculty for orderly thinking is in the pale of Saturn, which rather bestows a leaning towards pessimism than to optimism. (Mercury in opposition to Saturn.)

In married life this trait manifests itself through unfounded diffidence, and this certainly does not contribute towards harmony. By and by there has been an improvement in this respect, and my wife has also learned to adapt herself more readily.

Every marital union must be thought of as a dispensation assigned to man by higher direction, with the objective that both partners should endeavor to educate and complement each other.

A word about the 'child problem.' At least 16 years ago, when I was still beginning my Astrological studies, I computed, corrected, and interpreted the Horoscope of my bride, my present wife. Thus far I found no reason to doubt the accuracy of corrections carried out by means of primary directions.

This is now the third year that the conception rule, as discovered by Frank Glahn, has proved itself perfectly dependable. (From this, of course, it does not show any evidence whether or not the wife has been pregnant since.)

Sixteen years ago I prophesied to my bride we would have four children, mostly boys. In the meantime we have had four children, only with the difference that they were mostly girls, not boys. What is the reason for this? I am inclined to think that even the nature of the sex at conception is previously determined by astral influences. It is likely the Moon was the determining factor. I investigated the birth of our four children, ranging in the ages from four to nine years. I computed backwards 272 days from the day of birth, and accordingly fixed the position of the Moon in the sign of Leo or sign of Aquarius as the day of conception, whichever position of the Moon was closest. The following was the result:

1. Child-daughter. Pregnancy 272 days.

Moon decreasing in Aquarius at time of conception.

2. Child-daughter. Pregnancy 269 days.
   Moon decreasing in sign of Aquarius at time of conception.

3. Child-son. Pregnancy 266 days.
   Moon increasing in sign of Leo at time of conception.

4. Child-daughter. Pregnancy 277 days.
   Moon increasing in sign of Aquarius at time of conception.

Apparently we have the following: The Moon at conception passing over the descendant (7th cusp of the horoscope) produced girls at birth in all these cases. In one case the Moon passing over the ascendant, at time of conception, a boy was born. In two instances the decreasing Moon at the time of conception brought on a female birth. The increasing Moon in one case a female, in the other a male."

I have added these statements for the event that young married people would want to make a contribution themselves, in registering the conception period, to verify whether or not the increasing Moon passing over the ascendant of the wife will indicate rather the birth of sons, or whether the decreasing Moon passing over the descendant of the horoscope of the wife will vouch for more daughters. It does not cost anything to try.

We realize, of course, that in our days of economic distress many more children are born unintentionally than consciously; and the families are quite rare which today are looking for many children.

There is another student of Astrology, who submitted his own Horoscope (Chart No. 13), that of his first wife (Chart No. 14), and that of his second wife (Chart No. 15), also that of his mother (Chart No. 17) for examination. At his own initiative he wrote the following:

"I would also like to give something without simply taking, and contribute something for astrology, love affairs, and the Reflectors ("Spiegelbilder"). On account of disturbances at my home and in my married life I had come to investigate astrology, striving to find "a way to discover myself" in books. I did not fancy much a life outside of my home at taverns and similar things. I was bound to search just why things are as they are, and why I failed to overcome fate in spite of the supreme summoning of all my nerves. (I had five court trials on account of marital troubles.)

In consequence of a shattered union, especially in the years 1919 and 1921, I came close to committing suicide. My mother is largely to blame for these ruptures, as she lived with me, and I made provisions for her since I was sixteen. She always attempted to dominate, with her violent and impulsive character, my first wife and myself, even though I was past thirty. When the first union broke up, and I married a second time, my mother interfered a second time with our marital affairs. But in this case I sided with my second wife, and gave my mother the choice either to move, to go into some old people's home, or to leave sole control to us. She preferred the first. Accordingly I have lived with my second wife for four years in the best of spirits. Our regret is that we have no children. The mother stays at the old people's home, is still spry and dominant at 75, but not on speaking terms with me nor with my sister. The latter had already known mother's dominant ways fifteen years ago, the meanwhile I had always tried to be unselfish and honor the fourth commandment.

The Horoscope will serve to give you a kaleidoscope of my life with its events."

In the first sections of this volume I have already referred to the respective Horoscope charts, and explained the planetary positions, inasmuch as they especially furnish proof. I leave it to the readers to draw subsequent conclusions of these, and to compare the Horoscopes with one another. Those that were separated from one another simply did not fit together, and we must remember here also, that one of the parties can hardly be blamed for everything. Conditions were hopeless in themselves, enough to undermine happy marriages. Nor would it be wise to allow the mother-in-law to interfere in marital matters. That the second union of the man (Chart No. 13) has been happier than the first, may easily be ascertained on the basis of astrological rules.

Fortunes & Love Tragedies

We also have a very interesting Horoscope of a very young woman, already divorced, in whose Horoscope Uranus is in the 7th house, but in triplicity to Jupiter in the 11th house. She will never lack admirers nor good friends.

A well known Astrological expert has described the character of the young woman as follows:

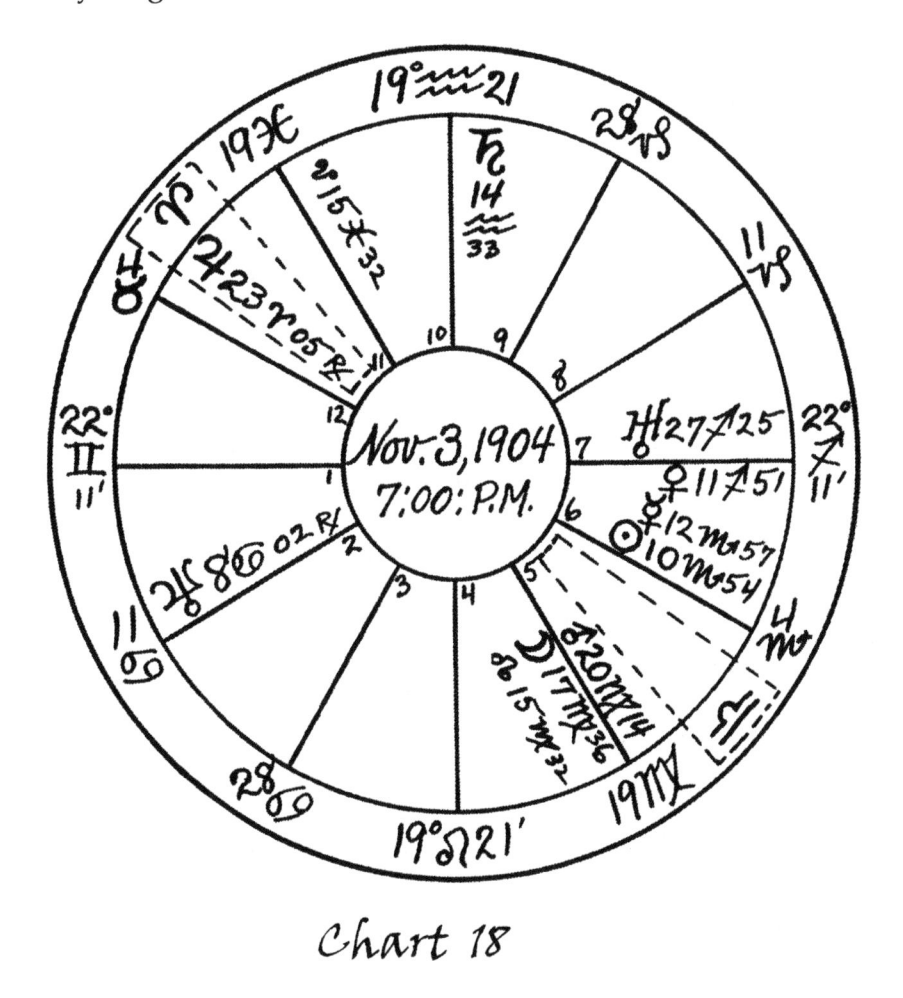

Chart 18

"Her disposition is of a strong, quickly changing, and incalculable type. On the one hand she quickly and firmly adapts herself to situations changing very suddenly, and she feels quite at home in prevailing conditions. On the other hand she is a slave to her own wants and vacillating whims. If she would exercise a strong self-control, that would help her over the unfavorable escapades of her temper.

In her emotional life she is of a conflicting temperament; there is a trend, a cleaving originally between her individually and her personality, and it is difficult to weld both together harmoniously. Viewed in this light this Horoscope does not represent the average person, but an eccentric human being, which either rises or descends, but never moves on a level.... The statement concerning marriage is complicated. A union is entered upon with facility, but none of her marriages would last long, they are being separated in court. The partner that is best assigned to her must be able to follow her startling, bounding caprices, he must be positively enterprising, and show connections with foreign countries. She may enter into business partnership only on a very loose basis and with such people as would engage in occult problems or modern industry. (Uranus in the 7th house in good aspect with Jupiter.) For a vocation there are good opportunities to apply her intellect, at best in the field of literature. Whatever she has of personal experiences would only react as a reproof for her vocation. Her finances would at the first undergo great vacillations, but later would be stabilized....

Her coterie of friends is advantageous, she knows how to use them at a great benefit for herself. She has no real enemies. Her dealings with servants and inferiors, and to the people in general, are quite propitious.

All travels are convenient for her constitution as well as for her vocation.

Her health is not very robust; there are indications of fevers and infections. Her throat, neck, heart and genital system will become diseased first. Much of outdoor life, sport activities, will favorably offset these proclivities. Her artistic and intellectual propensities will prove to be of great value for her literary productions and for her success, though she is mystically inclined."

As far as I know the young lady personally, the description is fitting, although I do not believe that all of her journeys will terminate successfully, since Saturn in the 9th house of her Horoscope also points to many silent disturbances of mind while traveling and in foreign countries, but that she will not show it. Very rarely I found a human being so distinctive and versatile in character, bubbling over with fun, but also reasonable, prudent, and logical in her expressions of thought. The young lady can analyze her own sentiments admirably. Concerning herself she wrote to me the following in a private letter for my collection:

"My name is Hedwig. It is an old German name. 'Hat' meant 'battle,' and as the interpretation for that became lost, 'wig' was added, which also means 'battle,' the 'display of vigor,' it thus means: 'battle-battle.' The name fits me, life is a battle to me, whether this is evident in thought or in action.

I am born November 3rd, 1904, 7 P.M. My youth was gay and carefree, and replete with changing friendships. I was engaged scarcely after leaving school, in 1922; my marriage was rather peculiar, as it was less of a marriage than a good friendship between my husband and myself.

Our characteristics, traits, sentiments and desires were contradictory. That which the one wanted, seemed to be remote for the other. In addition I was intensely anxious to derive out of life what I could. I wanted to know everything, see and experience everything, participate and live in it, and not miss a thing. Towards this end I wanted a mature leader who would establish contact, choose and sift, inasmuch as many impressions received will retard development, and are no aid for progress. My husband was very young (born May 20th, 1899) and was unable to lead. In the course of these two years I had the urge to be far removed from him. I fretted, became nervous and ill; I was dissatisfied with myself, and I longed for everything.

Good friends there were, I always have them (Jupiter in the 11th house of the horoscope); perhaps they gave too much thought to me and aroused my attention to diversified objects. My ideas became confused, my thoughts discordant. I was happy to engage in literary work, into which I rushed as intensively as I did into all things with which I occupied my mind.

I was told that I dissipated too much time upon vanities, and at high speed of living spent my best energies. That may be; up to date I do not realize it. This may be strange; there is nothing that will deter me, and I usually succeed. Nevertheless I am fearful at times, worried about my life. I falter at every danger, and presence of mind is far removed from me.

My husband and I separated after a union lasting hardly two years, although it was hard to do. But our marriage had become senseless, and it was necessary to end it. To this day I am very much attached to him, much as I cannot ever be separated from any person with whom I had become intimate. I need the love and affection of all people with whom I come in contact, as much as anybody else, in order to feel good and be happy.

This much I know today, my life will not move along in a closed circle; there will be many minor and ever recurring courses, a struggle, a quick victory, a craving for that which is new, only to be as quickly disappointed, and to begin all over again. Sometimes I look at the swirl of my life from the outside until I get dizzy, and then I straightway plunge into it again, yes, again and again, and I twirl along with it."

In this autobiography the traits are reflected which are bestowed by the ascendant sign of Gemini and the influence of the Sun in Scorpio. The Moon also, in the sign of Virgo in conjunction with Mars, has a strong influence.

There is another interesting Horoscope, giving much information (Chart No. 19), with the Sun in the sign of Scorpio in conjunction with Saturn, Mars, and Uranus in the sign of Scorpio in the death house. It is that of a young man, still unmarried, whose fortunes are quite remarkable. He hails from a respected family, was adjutant in a first-rank position in war, became buried in the debris, was saved, as it were, by a miracle, and has again risen from the dead. But he does not feel happy at all, since the inflation left him as poor as a church mouse, and he could not obtain work that suited him.

This peculiar character, influenced by the Sun and several planets in Scorpio, was prevailed upon to write to me something

Fortunes & Love Tragedies

about his love affairs, and he submitted the following confession:

"Railroad and ship carried me from country to country, from city to city, from town to town. Also from ... woman to woman, beginning from the subdued conversation, under the glittering luster of light, with overstrung noblewomen down to the noisy dilly-dallying with painted faces in taverns that were hazy with tobacco smoke.

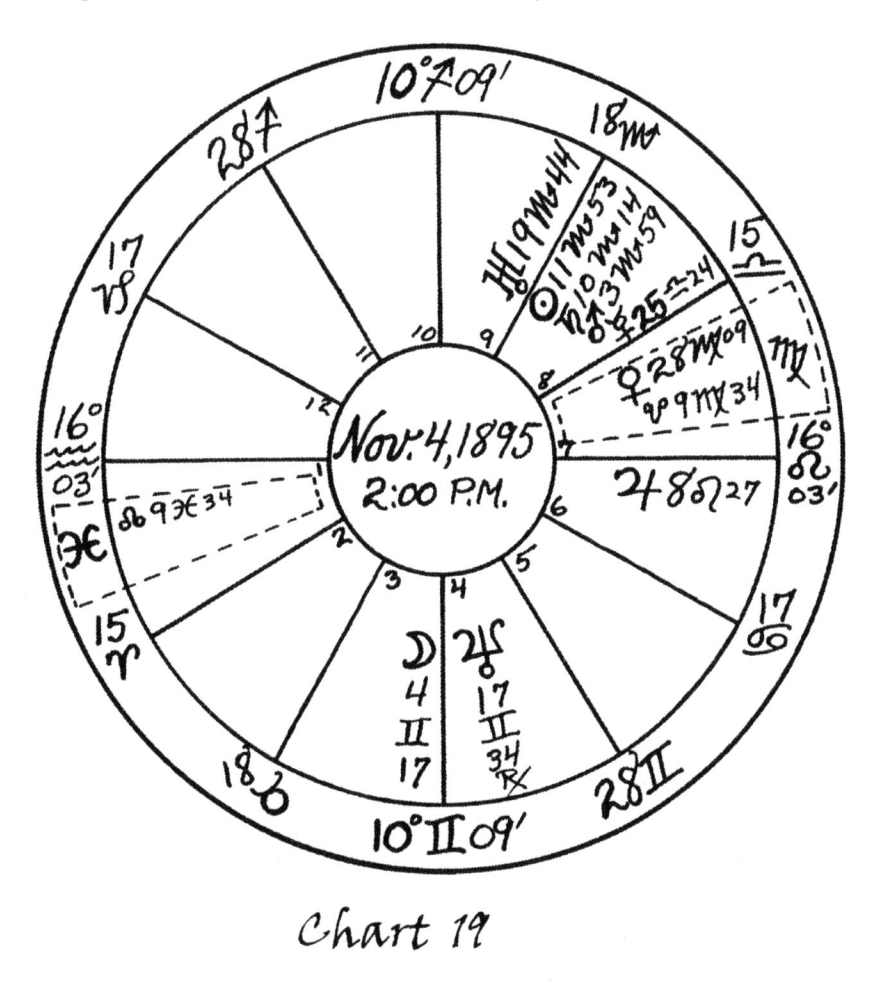

Chart 19

Whether they were blonds, brunettes or red heads, it was all the same to me. I would escort them to some elegant home, or to the miserable room in the attic. Above all I preferred to bring them to my quarters. All of them, without exception, were prevailed upon to confess-their life, their sins, their good deeds, and the object of their longing.

All these girls and women became quite frank in my presence, entirely so. Perhaps they felt that I had an unlimited faculty for understanding, for comfort and forgiveness, and that I could and would give much of wholesome advice. They became candid in their utterances, except that those who were sensual were on their guard.

If you want to witness a film which often unraveled itself in the course of my life, then listen. She was on the street, at midnight, when I saw her for the first time. Her dejected appearance caused me to look at her. Without a word I beckoned her, and without a word she joined in the walk. Would she talk? Or venture at jokes, or demand, or act? To be sure. But she uttered not a sound.

For many years, until a short time ago, my rooms were fitted out in Russian style. That puts one into a singular mood, my mood. The samovar (phonograph) dreamily hummed melodies of bygone days. On a spacious divan she lay buried in pillows, the creature of the street. Her torn shoes she had exchanged, at my behest, with padded slippers, and the street dress, ruined by the rain, was replaced with a black house dress which a Russian friend had given me some time ago. The grayish blue smoke of the popoff cigarette hovered lazily over the woman, and assumed grotesque forms. I did not smoke. I sat in front of her on a wide divan, arranging cups, sugar, milk, rum and arrak. A utility table was brought, and I spread butter on bread slices, also brought some sweets. I then handed her a bank note which she took without a word. I leaned back in my chair, gazed at the smoke that gathered beneath the shade of the floor lamp, and a subdued conversation was entered upon:

At first the girls and women would eat, later their eyes would look surprised, then again there was something revolving in their mind and finally, tears were shed. That varied according to their respective disposition. I know full well how to distinguish the genuine from the make-believe; it is my nature that wants it so. Experience is not enough. I can rely upon my intuitive divining faculty. I continued to speak until real tears came. Then I waited. Again I added a few words, and begged.

My entreaty was fulfilled in every instance, and I heard

confessions. Here, too, I felt what was true and what was garnished. The film has come to a stop.

There was only one lewd woman (was she really bad or only normal?) that I had become acquainted with. All the rest, which "society" (making the startling claim to be better) calls bad, were thrown upon their course through dire want, through hunger, the hunger of their mothers, and through disreputable men who made sport of honor. That women do not return from these conditions is the fault of the prejudice of men and the struggle of making a living.

Of the women whom I found beneath the chandelier I received their confession amidst laughter and levities.

Thus my spirit and its place of repose, my temper, has discovered and divined many a woman, and that is better, a thousand times better, than that my body should have felt that of the woman.

In the course of all these confessions and conversations I was filled with sorrow for humanity, and with an understanding for its cheerlessness, its superficiality, falseness, and indolence; I learned to know the modern man. Accordingly, I understand the saying which has given so much to me, and which I cherish: 'Children, dear children, love one another!'

This may be about six years since I am living a new kind of love. Formerly I returned many a girl to her parents of which she had been cast off, or which had been considered lost. I have returned many a wife to her husband. But I have also come to the realization in the last few years that this kind of trouble would be entirely useless in modern times. Moreover, my mind craved for food other than these confessions. I searched for a different kind of charity, and I found it.

If you would view a film concerning this, then listen again:

A wide space, furnished with Rococo furniture with dark blue velvet. In the French fireplace there are red flames hopping and gliding over crackling pine logs. In a comfortable chair next to the fireplace there is a delicate woman. Her hair, braided in old fashion, has the tint of fresh snow, and the softness of Chinese silk. The dainty shoes are half hidden in an enormous pillow of blue velvet, and the delicate hands play in my hair.

We gaze into the flames, and softly there comes from the lips of the fine woman a tale of distant countries, of the glamorous period at the court of Napoleon, concerning a happy home, concerning God, our Lord.... My turn is next. I laugh and weep, I make poetry and dream, I shout for joy and sigh, confess and pray.

In gratitude for such varieties of my love I was permitted to stay sound in health.

To be healthy -- that was the first stage.

Almost unconsciously, it is but natural, I search for a woman, just for myself, the woman. I searched with my mind. Meanwhile I permitted it to be submerged into my temper. I had a new experience, I developed step for step. The mind widened, the temper deepened, the tension increased between mind and soul. This was not changed as I was obliged otherwise that was automatic, my second self, to memorize long theses and pass uninteresting examinations. Gradually I became strong.

Strong -- that was the second stage.

I am sound and strong, and now I lift up my foot to climb to the third stage. It is the last and supreme. The spirit alone will lead to it. A mallet has engraved the words on it: 'The spirit alone is not limited by space and time.' I rely upon my spirit. It has the power to lift the body into the goal. On to the last stage, where I hope to find all fellow-men:

'Healthy, strong, and happy!' "

Such is the confession of this man, and still in a faltering mood he complains again and again that there is no use for him to try, since he has no one that loves him, or for whom he ought to provide. The many planets in the 8th house of the Horoscope direct his thought too much towards the end, so that life's battles do not seem to him worth while.

Fortunes & Love Tragedies

We find a disposition happier by nature with the female (Chart No. 20) born December 3rd, 1885, at whose birth the Sun was in the sign of Sagittarius, with the sign of Libra rising in the east, so that Venus is ruler of life. Jupiter, being close to the ascendant in the sign of Libra, gave her a kind and philanthropic turn of mind, attractiveness and amiability. Since, however, the ruler or chief planet of the 7th house, (Aries) is the impetuous Mars in the 12th

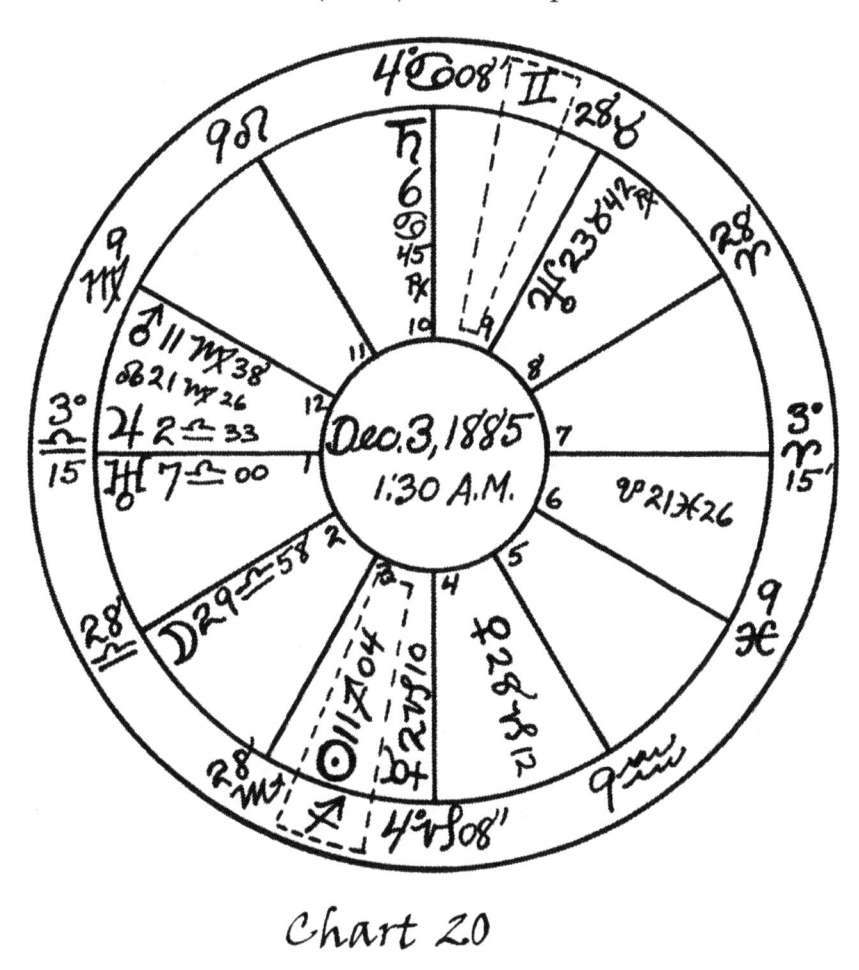

Chart 20

house, which deals with enemies, throws a quartile upon the Sun, it is not surprising she is constantly perturbed in her mind in dealing with men, and that her marriage is not a success. She still looks youthful and well preserved; notwithstanding sad experiences she is always full of life and wistful. She writes as follows:

"Although I am not in the position to interpret my own horoscope, I am satisfied, nevertheless, inasmuch as I received your annual for 1926, which I had anticipated during the entire fall season. I should like to remind you from the very beginning of the case of the movie actress you know. On Page 109 of your 'Vision of the Future,' it is shown that apparently she had the same experience as I had, since she is influenced by the sign of Sagittarius, even as I, and also married one born in the sign of Gemini. The difference between her and myself is that I will never return, and that I would have nothing to do any more with one ruled over by the sign of Gemini. In the beginning one may expect only the best imaginable of such people; however, this does not last long, and later there is no other possibility but to separate as soon as possible, that is the only salvation. Whenever Sagittarius types come together with Gemini types, they are lost, whether they want to be or not.

Now I am going to tell of my life, beginning of 1913, since my unhappy experiences began in that year.

I am born December 3rd, 1885, 1:30 A.M., at Munich, and am under the influence of Sagittarius, also of Jupiter and Venus. These are very nice planets, but they leave much to be desired.

The day must have been a Thursday.

From 1911 to 1913 I was very happy; during this time I was engaged to a doctor of Würzburg. In September, 1913, he went to Trier (Treves) on furlough, and died there in October, 1913, with a stroke, two months before the designated date of the wedding.

At my home in Bamberg I then became acquainted with a very good man. He was drafted and fell as early as August 14th, 1914. I went to Munich, and fate would have it that I fell victim to a crook. We only had a court wedding at Munich. I at once entered plea for nullification, and at the close of 1914 my marriage was declared void by law. My maiden name was returned to me. I remained in the same building for a time. In a peculiar way I became acquainted with an artist who was older and better. It so happened that I was advertising our large dog for sale, and the artist referred to wanted to buy him. We thus accidentally learned of each other, and our relations lasted for three years, until 1918. Mars separated us. The man was born May 1st, 1876. From 1916 I was in the Red Cross, and I went to the front until 1918; up to March, 1919, I was engaged in a hospital. I was a good nurse, and I wished I would have stayed there. At Munich fate persecuted me a second time. Through some acquaintances I met an orderly sergeant, George W., of the staff of the Seventh Division. He was born June 9th, 1891. This man destroyed all my happiness, and my good career. To this day I am under his spell; I am also legally obligated because of alimony I was receiving from him. Our wedding was on October 8th, 1919, at Munich. At first our union was quite happy, but the wind soon turned. Our married life became a hell. Never again would I want to suffer as much, it is something frightful that I stood for. We were already at odds in 1920 and 1921, living separated. I went to B. Divorce proceedings were conducted while I was still at Munich. Mr. W. made application twice for a divorce; each time he was refused, until I made application. We were thus divorced September 22nd, 1922, the verdict being that the man was guilty on account of adultery with Frieda W. He had met this Frieda in 1920; both were quite happy and wanted to marry, before we were divorced.

Miss W. is born June 17th, 1895; she had been engaged to a paymaster, from whom she received a great deal of money. This money she used up with my husband, and she supported him. W. knew of the affairs of Frieda, but that did not bother him. This woman made of him a moral derelict, so that there is nothing good about him any more.

Why must this be; why must I thus be tormented? Ever since 1919 and to this day I have my troubles, and the pleasant years are gone. This will be seven years in October that I am grieved; I am afraid of a third union, and yet I do not care to remain single.

My father died June 20th, 1918. Since that time there is no peace in the house any more with the rest of the family, it is simply frightful. (Mercury third house in opposition to Saturn.)

My mother is born April 14th, 1852; she is strongly influenced by Aries. Thus there are many conflicts. My brothers and my sisters are influenced by the signs Gemini, Leo, Pisces, Virgo, and none of us get along well. Last summer I had a good friend, whose birthday is December 17th. We understood each other quite well, but my envious sisters spoiled it, as they had often done. What shall become of me? I am not yet abandoning hope of more pleasant days, that is my only consolation."

This confession shows that the life of those influenced by the sign of Sagittarius is unsettled and changeable. In this case other planetary configurations must be considered, carefully consult the Horoscope No. 20. If Mars would not be so hostile to the Sun, life would be more agreeable.

As a counterpart of the woman who is disposed to marry again in spite of her unhappy unions, I am presenting a Horoscope and a biography of one who had an insuperable aversion against marriage or any contact with men. The woman referred to writes as follows:

"I began my life November 24th, 1886, 1:30 P.M., in Suabia (Chart No. 21), being the fourth and last child of my parents. Shortly before I was born my father died as the result of a bad fall. When I was a little more than four years of age my mother was attacked by the owner of a mill, who wanted to marry her, but whom she could not love in return, and murdered. That was on March 27, 1891, early in the morning. (My mother was born March 19th, 1860, the hour I do not know.) I still have the memory of the gruesome sight of the murdered mother, as small as I was. Since my parents had no sisters or brothers, and my mother's father died two days after that incident, and my grandmother was too old, I was given to an old couple, who accepted me because of the board money. The severity of the foster-mother made of me an affrighted creature, afraid and apprehensive of men. A severe look gave me palpitation of the heart. Doctors who later examined me said that my heart trouble was due to rough treatment. No one showed any love to me, but everybody pitied me. No one learned of my grief, or that I was so utterly forsaken. I pleaded with the four walls and with my dear dead mother. When I had attained the 14th year I was assigned by my pastor and the guardian to a monastery for the purpose of additional instruction and education. The years of 1900 to 1905 were gay and happy for me. Every merciful sister wanted to take the place of my mother. One of them remained a motherly friend to me until she died in 1915. As I was a poor orphan I chose as my life's calling to take care of these helpless creatures. I thus decided to enter the normal school at Menzingen, Switzerland, as a missionary candidate, in the spring

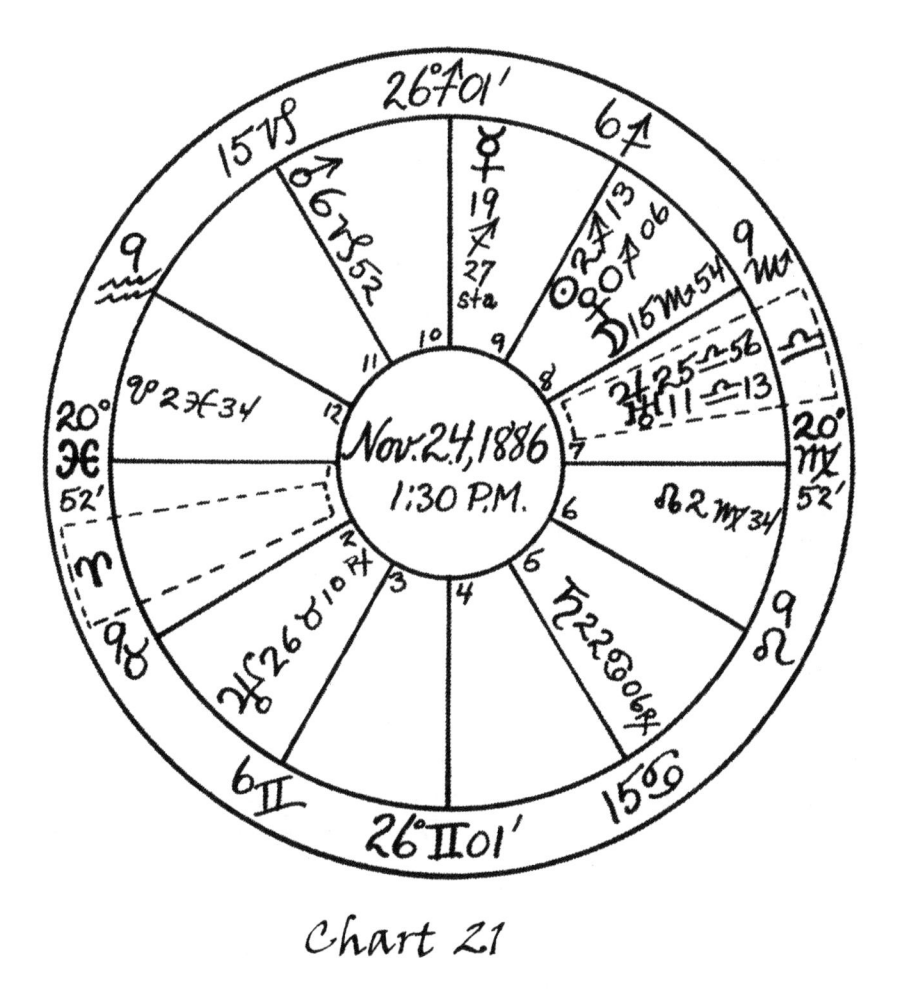

Chart 21

of 1905. When I had spent two years at that institute I was obliged to leave, because I was not strong enough for an exacting calling such as this. I left the cloisterlike solitude and plunged into life's hostility, though inexperienced and innocent like a child. Of worldly love I had not the least idea, and it seemed very difficult to me to espouse any other calling but that of charity. When I had passed the twentieth year of life I entered into a book store, and here, too, I was quite satisfied. Although I was not as secluded here as in the cloister, I did not experience at any time any love towards the other sex. It seemed as though from my very childhood I was filled with fear and horror of men ever since the tragic end of my mother. To this day I cannot entertain any particular sympathy for menfolk; I would rather die than to belong to some man."

How are we to explain all this?

The rising sign or the ascendant of this Horoscope is the sign of Pisces, which, as we know, bestows a weak constitution and renders extremely receptive to all influences. These people wish to help and to serve everywhere, when an opportunity presents itself, but they are often knocked around by external influences. They are not counted among the happy human beings, but always live under a baneful spell which compels them to stay in the background. They are battling continuously against mishaps of every description.

This astrological rule holds good also in this case; the woman born under this sign of Pisces thus far has had no easy life of it. She had been weighed down from childhood, with the exception of the peaceful years in the cloister, and has had her generous share of disappointments.

The chief planet or ruler of the sign of Pisces is Neptune, which is almost directly opposite to Venus and to the Sun in this Horoscope, and is significant for the tragic fate of the parents. In this Horoscope it is remarkable that Jupiter is in quartile to Saturn, and Uranus in quartile to Mars, thus indicating that this person will be greatly hampered in life.

This Horoscope again proves that planets in the 7th house, referring to either Uranus or Jupiter, do not bring any happiness at all into love affairs or married life, whenever they are opposed, as is the case here, by sharp quartiles of Saturn and Mars.

The person referred to, as she has told me herself, had several chances to marry in her younger days, as Sun and Moon in the bicorporeal sign of Sagittarius indicate this, but since the men courting her would not rest satisfied with a "Platonic" love, each

Fortunes & Love Tragedies

courtship came to an end.

Venus as "the bearer of happiness" stands in this Horoscope also in the house of death in an exact quartile to the Moon's north and south nodes, and, as has already been stated, in opposition to Neptune. Inasmuch as Uranus in the 7th house is in quartile to Mars, and the Sun is in opposition to Neptune, this will not be auspicious in the future for happiness in love and marriage; in fact, the person referred to does not ask for it.

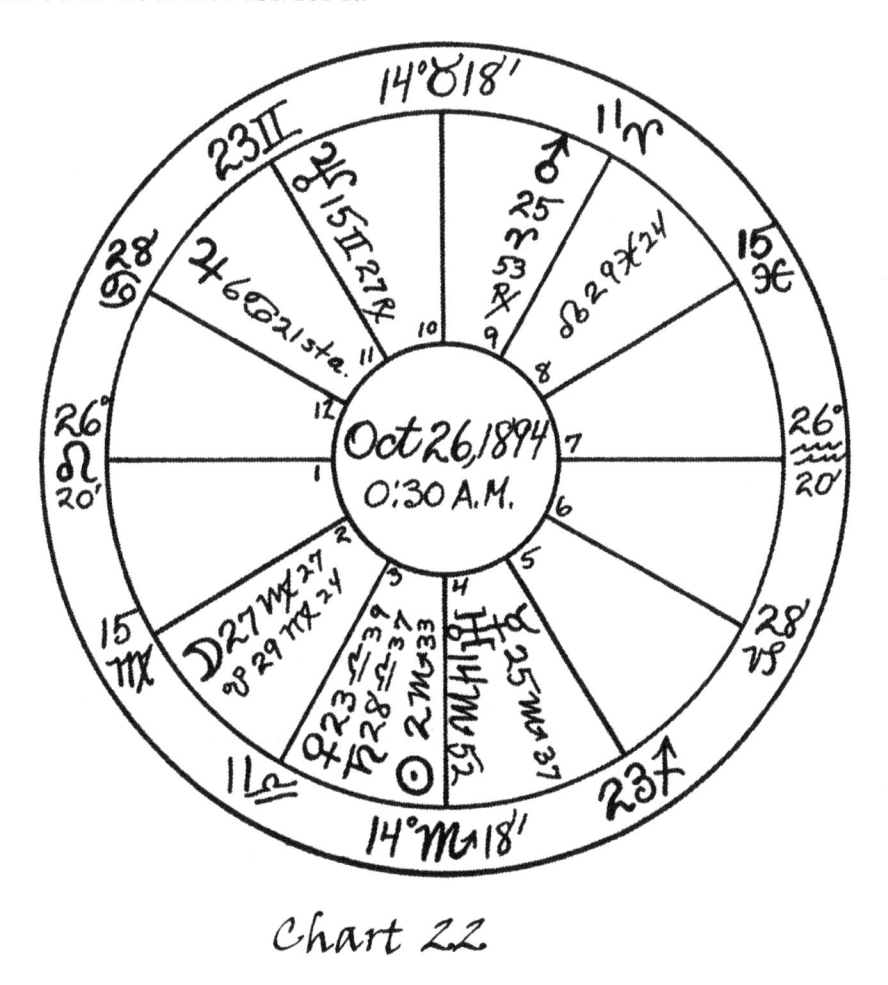

Chart 22

She has transferred all her devotions to animals, and thus much prefers to be alone with her pet cat.

We know of a counterpart to this alleged misanthrope, a

bachelor who would like to marry and establish a nice home of his own, and yet does not succeed in doing so despite his endeavors. He is born October 26th, 1894, 0:30 A.M. (Chart No. 22), and for many years he has constantly been on the search for a good and suitable wife.

Several times he had been seriously engaged, but, due to the conjunction of Venus and Saturn, he toned down in his affections towards the fiancée, and "someone else" was preferred. Mars in opposition to Venus and Saturn did his share in spoiling matters.

The ruler of the 7th house of this Horoscope, which begins in the last degrees of the sign of Aquarius, is Uranus, which is located at the fourth cusp, and it is remarkable that there were always affairs of the home and the family which opposed any and all agreements.

Nor does the Moon in conjunction with its south node favor the establishment of a cozy home.

Thus, to be sure, there is many a person yearning for permanent happiness in love and marriage, and in spite of all searching and hoping he cannot find it, if nature does not decree it so. All the examples referred to show that even with the aid of the stars one cannot grasp at happiness in love and marriage. Only this may be ascertained, whether or not, and when, one may expect happiness or good fortune, or whether the life of a person will run a more serious and tragic course. However, even the saddest fate will not be without its joys and elevating hours, since everything will come to pass according to a higher law in a manner in which it is best for the children of men.

Thus I shall close the volume with the words:

"With every happiness remember its end,
With every sorrow, that it will pass over."

FINIS